I0540695

WRONG ONES IN THE DOCK

T. M. ALUKO

The African Writers Series (AWS) is a collection of books written by different African novelists, poets and politicians. Initially Published by Heinemann Educational Books Limited. The Collection contains more than 359 books.

ISBN: 978-1-957076-78-2

© T. M. Aluko 1982

First published by Heinemann Educational Books Ltd 1982

Chief Editor Chinua Achebe for African Writers Series © 1982

Second Edition by NEOBOOKS © 2026

Edited & Reprint by NEOBOOKS © 2026

Neoancestories@gmail.com

Part of the Original African Writer Series Collective Books: Book 242

CONTENTS

To Jacob

whose needless suffering inspired the writing of this novel

ONE

Jonathan was in trouble. My uncle Papa Ota had dreamed and seen Jonathan in chains in his dream. Whenever Papa Ota dreamt in the potent hours midway between midnight and cock-crow in the morning, his dream invariably came true with dreadful accuracy. And the dreams of my uncle invariably forebode evil.

I cut short my visit to him at Ota and started on the journey back to Lagos, still hoping for the best but preparing my mind for the worst. To be seen in chains in one of his dreams meant being in handcuffs in real life.

Just what could Jonathan have done that could have led to his being handcuffed by the police? He would not hurt a fly. Indeed, he was the biblical type who, if smitten on one cheek, would turn the other to his adversary. He was essentially a man of peace; therefore, the possibility of his being involved in violence was most remote. Unless, of course, he was the victim of such violence. In that case, he would have been taken to hospital and not taken away by the police as my uncle's dream had suggested.

Also, he was a most honest person who would not steal a penny. Indeed, his exemplary honesty was again and again cited to his colleagues in our organization whenever they were being reprimanded for pilfering fuel or falsifying claims for local purchases. It was unthinkable that the police had taken him away for fraud. Not Jonathan.

Could he have been involved in the counterfeit currency printing racket? Or in money doubling? Again, while he shared with all human beings the desire to have more money, he would not get mixed up with counterfeit currency dealers and money doublers. God knows he could do with more than his salary as a driver in the Housing Authority to feed his large family. But Jonathan was emphatically not the criminal type.

I was in the middle of these thoughts when I had to screech to a sudden stop to avoid running into the rear of a minibus that had halted very suddenly in front of me, knocking down a road diversion sign in the process. Its coming to a sudden stop had caused its passengers to pitch into one another and to panic, with yells and curses and prayers mixed together in a terrific din.

I got out of my car full of fury. I demanded to know the reason why the driver had driven so badly.

"Driven badly! Na abuse dis Oga de abuse me," the driver replied, eyeing me with insolent suspicion.

"Why were you driving so recklessly?" I insisted, my rage mounting. I was not only angry,

I was shaken. It was only my presence of mind that had saved us all from a nasty accident.

"Bo Oga. You no praise me self say I apply brake quick-quick," the driver argued. "If not for say I apply brake quick-quick, you no know say na different story we be telling now?"

"Perhaps you think you should be congratulated then—given a medal for driving so very well?"

"You no see say if I no sabby brake quick-quick, Oga..."

"Master, listen to me," one of the passengers said, tapping me on the shoulder. I turned to him. He was a lean man, with what looked like a broken jaw. He had a gold chain round his neck and wore an expensive lace agbada. But for his bad jaw, he appeared respectable. I found it surprising that such a superior-looking person should be riding in that killer vehicle.

"Master, what are we quarrelling about?" he asked.

"Quarrel! Who's quarrelling?" I asked, decidedly angry. "You saw how your driver drove recklessly?"

"It's the foolish roads people. Dem Ministry of Works labourers," the driver wailed. "They spoil the road. They go put sign board for corner-corner."

"Master, listen to me. Leave the driver alone," the man with the bad jaw said. I heeded his advice to look at him. His bad jaw was most probably the legacy from a previous motor accident.

"Master, you are not hurt. I am not hurt. And no one is hurt," he continued.

"Thanks to God, Jehovah," one woman said in gratitude to the Lord Jehovah because she and her fellow passengers were safe.

"So master, let the driver go," the man with the bad jaw insisted.

"But, but, but..." I stopped what I was going to say when I noticed a man in police uniform. Apparently, he was a passenger in the minibus.

"And what are you doing about this, constable?" I asked, taking three steps towards him.

"Me, sir?" the constable asked, looking surprised.

"Yes, you. What are you doing about this man?"

"What am I doing about him, sir?" the constable repeated blankly.

"This bad driver. This man that has driven so badly. Aren't you going to do something about him? For a start, do you see those tyres?" I said excitedly, as I moved to the vehicle indicating the two rear tyres. Neither had a tread and the foundation canvas was showing in three places on one of them.

"The tyres, sir?" the constable asked looking, like everyone else, at the tyres.

"Yes, the tyres. And what about his driver's licence and his roadworthiness certificate?" I was certain the scoundrel had neither. At best he might have an expired licence.

"Me, sir?" the constable asked, uneasily.

"Yes, you. Shouldn't you check such things after witnessing this man's reckless driving?"

"But Oga, I beg you. I'm not on duty," the constable declared. He walked away from me and the rest of the group towards the wing wall of a nearby culvert. On this he sat himself, facing away from me and the crowd.

I refused to be beaten. I moved towards him. "Is it not your duty, as an officer of the peace, to see that this villainous driver is apprehended? Is it not your duty as an officer of the peace to see that a man who has damaged government property is made to pay for it? Is it, is it..."

"All people come and see my trouble now," the constable wailed to the other passengers. "I tell this Oga that I am not on duty. Yet he wants to make trouble for me. Oga, I beg you. Please leave me alone," he cried.

"Master, Master..."

I turned round to see the owner of the female voice. She wore a white lace buba over a blue velvet iro. Everything about her was suggestive of a woman about town, the lady contractor type.

"Master," she repeated. "You are safe. And we are all safe, not so?"

I stared at her, without answering her question. But another woman did, saying: "Thanks to Jehovah," and, spreading her hands in an attitude of prayer, gazing skyward. "Jehovah God, I thank you," she repeated.

"Master, let the driver go," the first woman pleaded. "Let the police constable go too. Leave them both. For my sake." And she smiled at me alluringly.

I smiled at her, a despondent smile which she mistook for my falling for her charms. At this stage everyone in the crowd joined in pressing me to abandon the case. In frustration I went back to my car; I manoeuvred it past the group and the minibus. Moments later I had reached a steady 80 kph, senselessly punishing the innocent car for the guilt of the driver who ought to have been punished, the officer of the law who refused to arrest him and the passengers who begged that both be left alone. I reflected on the society we live in. A society in which men and women see public property being damaged by reckless drivers and yet elect to take sides with the driver when there is the chance of bringing him to book. Yet all the people in that bus knew that the damaged property was being financed from their own taxes. Imagine a society in which a law enforcement officer in uniform refused to use the law against a criminal and excused himself by saying that he was not on duty! I found it difficult to understand that the passengers could plead for erring drivers without realizing that they, or their relatives, could be the next victims of these potential killers.

I remembered then what an expatriate police superintendent had once told me in his deep Scottish accent about the incorrigibility of drivers. "Look, I want to tell you something," he had said. "Those drivers are bastards. They are not Nigerians at all. They belong to another race. They do not even belong to the human race."

"Where do they come from then?" I had asked him, amused.

"Where do they come from? From hell. That's where they come from. And I swear I'll see they all get back to hell by the time I finish with them." And indeed he saw many drivers to gaol before he was hounded out of the country.

Jonathan was a driver for the Lagos Housing Authority. He was so different from the normal run of drivers that my friend the police superintendent would have put him in a class by himself. He was certainly the safest of the drivers in the organization. On several occasions the

General Manager had asked him to drive him whenever his official chauffeur was away ill, or on leave. But now, unfortunately, Jonathan was in trouble because my uncle Daniel, Papa Ota, had dreamt that he was in trouble. And, I repeat, whenever my uncle Papa Ota dreamt bad dreams, they usually meant trouble.

TWO

Jonathan was truly in trouble. My wife Bola confirmed the fact as soon as I got home.

"There has been trouble here," she said.

"Not Jonathan, Bola?" I asked, apprehensively.

"Yes, Jonathan. But how did you know?"

"Papa Ota told me. He dreamt that Jonathan was in chains. What, what has happened?"

"He is in police custody. Arrested for fighting," Bola said, impressed by the accuracy of Papa Ota's dream.

"Jonathan involved in a fight? Incredible."

"I was surprised too, but you don't have to shout so much," Bola said.

"Jonathan, fighting? I don't believe it." Jonathan just wasn't the fighting type. Jonathan was a man of peace. "The whole thing still sounds strange and vague. There are no details of what happened."

"No details? But Jonathan? Where's he now?"

"I told you, he has been arrested by the police. Raliatu sent one of her daughters to say that her husband has been arrested. The girl gave no details at all."

"Why has Raliatu herself not been here to tell us what's happened to her husband?" I asked.

"I don't know. You know how she is."

Yes, I knew. Raliatu was a devoted wife and loving mother, in many respects. But easily confused. Quite obviously the incident had taken her beyond her depth.

"Which of the daughters came, Bola?"

"Alice."

"Well, surely she is old enough to know what happened. She should be sensible enough to know what happened and where her people are."

"She said she was away at school. When she came back the house was deserted. She said some friend of hers living two houses away told her that there had been a serious fight and that her father had been arrested by the police."

"And her mother?"

"I've told you the girl had no more information. I think Raliatu just ran away from the house after the police took her husband away. No doubt she has escaped to one of her husband's relatives."

Bola and I debated for some time whether to go and look for Jonathan, or to go and look for Raliatu. If Jonathan was with the police he could be in any of three police stations on the Mainland. Not knowing exactly which one of the three could mean frustrating motoring through the evening traffic congestion, going from one police station to another. Besides, there was the possibility that Jonathan, arrested by the police the night before, could have been released already, without our knowing. The better course of action, we decided, was to go and look for Raliatu, who would have up-to-date information about her husband's trouble.

Bola made me eat something before we set out. As we inched our way through the traffic in Bola's car I still found difficulty in believing that Jonathan could have been involved in a fight or that he had been arrested by the police. We discussed their motive for arresting him.

"Breach of the peace," I suggested as a possible but unlikely charge.

"What does that mean?" Bola asked.

"What it says. Wrongful interference with the normal peaceful atmosphere which exists in a locality, and which all the residents can lawfully expect to enjoy," I said, with the importance of one belonging to the learned profession.

Bola immediately saw the shallowness of my definition. "Then the proprietors of those shops that advertise gramophone records and tapes by playing them on loudspeakers should be arrested." I laughed.

"And the Imam in the mosque who wakes everyone up at 5 am every day by going on the loudspeaker and reciting the Koran. Why do they do that?"

"Why? Calling the faithful to prayer," I said, trying to squeeze through a small opening between my lane and the lane of traffic coming from the opposite direction. Good old Beetle. It is master of the road in these tight conditions.

"Then according to you both the man who sells gramophone records and the Imam in the mosque are breachers of the peace. They should be arrested because both of them interfere with the peaceful atmosphere which all the residents of a locality can expect to enjoy," she said logically and triumphantly.

"They should be arrested," I agreed, even though I knew that these two could hardly come under the definition of a breach of the peace. Catch our police going to the mosque to arrest the Imam!

"And what are the other possibilities that could have landed Jonathan in police custody?"

"Assault."

"Assault and battery?"

"Yes, assault and battery."

"What does that mean?"

"What it means? Assaulting a fellow human being, and causing him bodily injury. Please don't ask me for the definition of the battery half of the thing."

"Look, look, look," Bola yelled, slamming her right foot on an imaginary brake where she sat. I had that very instant pressed hard on the proper footbrake. I swerved sharply to my left. It was made necessary by the sudden appearance of a motorcycle which, emerging from a lane between two houses on the street we were on, proceeded to speed along the road—in the wrong direction. I had narrowly missed a head-on collision with it.

"He's mad," I cried, as, through my rear mirror, I watched the progress of the motorcycle in the wrong direction. "Mad? He's a criminal," Bola cried, furiously.

"It happens all the time. Motorcyclists weaving in and out of traffic, completely unmindful of the rule to keep to the correct lane. Remember that motorcyclist in Montgomery Road?" I asked her.

"Terrible," she said in awful recollection of an accident which, but for the grace of God, could have been serious. She had been driving that same Beetle, with our little daughter at her side.

She had entered Montgomery, a one-way street, from Murtala Mohammed Way. At that same time a motorcycle emerged from Montgomery Road and entered Murtala Mohammed Way in the wrong direction! Her sudden application of the brake had pitched the little girl into the windscreen, which was shattered. And the offending motorcyclist had continued his journey completely unconcerned about what had happened.

We parked the Beetle some hundred metres away from Jonathan's house. Fasanya Street where he lived was bad for cars, thanks to the innumerable craters in the middle of the road. The Local Government Council were inadequate, hopelessly inadequate, to the task of keeping this and the many other roads in the area in good repair.

A relation of Jonathan's called Gregory lived in the nether regions of the house in front of which we parked. I sent a small boy to call him out.

"Welcome master," he greeted me when he came out. "Ah, madam. Welcome, madam," he said, when he discovered that Bola was in the car.

"You well, Gregory?" I asked him.

"I'm well, master. But you have heard about Jonathan, master?" he asked excitedly.

"Yes," I told him, as I locked the car. "We've come to see what happened."

"Oh, I come with you, master."

"Yes, do."

"Let me call a boy to watch your car, master. Ben, Ben, Ben—" he cried. No reply. "But you Celia, you hear me calling Ben and you don't help me call him. Foolish girl. You come here yourself. Sit down here and watch this car. I go to Papa Paul's house." Paul was the son of Jonathan.

"What happened, Gregory?" I asked him again, as all three of us walked down the road. Unfortunately, the pedestrian traffic was heavy, so talking and walking at the same time was difficult. I suggested that we step aside in front of a vacant plot, where we could talk uninterrupted.

"Yes?"

"Master, it was big trouble we saw here," he began.

"Yes?"

"Big trouble, master. I myself, I went to work. When I came back I was told that there was big, very big fight."

"Yes?" I wanted the details, not the preliminaries.

"And Jonathan was taken away by the police."

"But, but did he fight?"

"No, he did not fight. Everybody there said Jonathan did not fight. It was two women in the house. They were fighting. It began when a girl abused a woman. The woman fought the girl. Then they said the mother of the girl fought the woman. Then the son of the first woman fought the other woman."

"But how did Jonathan come into all this?"

"They said Paul fought the son of the first woman."

"Yes?"

"And Jonathan was separating Paul and Gilbert."

"Gilbert? Who's Gilbert?" I asked.

"Gilbert is the son of the first woman who was fighting the other woman. Jonathan was separating Paul and Gilbert. They said Gilbert wanted to hit Paul with an axe. But by mistake the axe hit his own mother. Then the mother fell."

"She fell—did she? Was she badly injured?"

"Everybody thought at first that she was dead. They called a taxi, which took her to the General Hospital at Ikeja. On the way to the hospital she opened her eyes. She is now receiving treatment in the hospital.

The brother of the husband of the woman had run to report to the police when it was thought that the woman had died. Then the police came to take all of them away, including Jonathan. Before we came back from the police station Raliatu had taken the children away from the house. They could not sleep in the place because of trouble."

"Jonathan is not with the police, then?" Bola asked.

"No. He came back from the police station," Gregory said. "Some people saw him when he came back in the night."

Bola and I exchanged glances of relief. Jonathan then was not in police custody.

"I think he has gone to look for Raliatu and the children. I don't know where they are. They are probably hiding with Raliatu's father at Mushin," Gregory told us.

"I see, I see," I observed, relieved.

"I think it's probably good that they should stay away for some time," Bola said. "Till tempers cool down."

"I think so, madam," Gregory said.

"When they come back tell Jonathan that I want to see him," I said.

"Yes, sir."

We decided all the same to move on to 22 Fasanya Street where Jonathan Egbor, Raliatu Egbor his wife, their two daughters and three sons—all seven of them occupied one single room on the ground floor of a two-storey house. It was the "face-me-I-face-you" type of house in which a one-metre wide corridor separated two rows of rooms, each the Lagos City Council by-law minimum size of four metres by three metres. The door of each room exactly faced on to the door of another room at the other side of the corridor.

In this particular house there were twelve rooms on each floor, six on each side of the corridor with the first two in each row communicating through an internal door to convert them into a room and parlour for the higher level of the low-income group for whom the buildings were normally designed.

"Good evening, Mr Nwanna," I greeted the man who occupied the room and parlour on the left side of the ground floor corridor.

"Good evening, sir," he replied. "Good evening, Mrs Banjo. How are the children?"

"Very well, thank you. And how's your wife?" Bola asked.

"Very well, madam."

"I hear you had trouble here yesterday, Mr Nwanna?"

"It was terrible, sir. Real terrible. The thing that our eyes saw here yesterday, sir. It was terrible."

"Just what happened?" I asked him.

"These people in this house. They fight too much. The children are always fighting one another. The women are always fighting one another. And one mother is always coming to the aid of her child."

"And one child is always coming to the aid of her mother," Bola said, with a chuckle.

"You understand the situation very well, madam," Nwanna told her.

"I suppose where so many people live in one compound like this, they will get in each other's way," I observed. "When all seven members of a family are crowded together in one room and have to share bath and toilet with members of other families—it must lead to serious friction. Terrible." I shuddered at the unbelievable overcrowding in the house. I knew that 22 Fasanya Street was no exception. It was a measure of the terrible overcrowding in Lagos.

"You understand the position too well, sir," Nwanna repeated. "The people are too many in each room. Far too many. They overflow into the corridor and the little compound outside. They move about the corridor like rabbits. And they litter the place like pigs. They are terrible, sir."

"It must be difficult for you, Mr Nwanna," Bola said. "I mean living with all these people. All the children yelling. And all the women fighting."

"Too difficult, madam. Too difficult. I am already looking for a new place. I pray that I get a new place before my wife comes back. I pray she doesn't return to this place."

"She is away then?" I asked.

"Yes, sir. She is away at the teacher training college at Umuahia."

"Oh that's good. Very good. But you were telling us about the fight," I steered him back to the relevant from the irrelevant.

"Yes, sir. I don't know how the trouble really started. I think two children were fighting at first. Then the mothers were fighting too. Then the two boys took over. In no time the place was in uproar."

"Which two boys, Mr Nwanna?" I asked.

"Gilbert and Paul, sir. We all tried to separate them. But they refused to listen. Even Papa Paul tried much to separate them. It was that mad boy they call Gilbert who put fuel in the trouble."

"Gilbert?" I said, recalling that Gregory had mentioned the name earlier.

"Yes. The son of the man who lives in the last room there. Papa Paul at first succeeded in separating the two of them. Then Gilbert came back with a stick and hit Papa Paul from behind."

"Why did he do that?"

"Why? He is mad. That's why. Everyone in this house knows that he is a drug addict. He is a criminal and his parents know that he will sooner or later go to gaol. That boy will go to prison one day. I'm sure."

"Did Jonathan hit him back?" I asked.

"Oh no. Not at all. He only asked everyone present to witness what the foolish boy had done and that he would report Gilbert to his father when he came back from work."

"That sounds more like Jonathan," I said to Bola.

"But Paul went to Gilbert and boxed him on the ear. And everyone thought it was a good thing too. That Gilbert boy needed someone to teach him a lesson. Good-for-nothing idiot. He aimed a blow at Paul with the stick in his hand, but people prevented him from striking the blow. I personally wrested the stick from his hand," Nwanna said.

"And did it all happen in this corridor?" I asked him.

"It started in the corridor, then continued in the compound out here," he said, indicating the air-space in which two motorcycles and a bicycle were parked. "They in fact damaged the headlamp of my motorbike. Foolish idiots. From here they came to the front of the house. In fact they caused much obstruction in the street."

"Really?"

"Yes, sir. But you know what that foolish boy did after I had taken the stick away from him?"

"What did he do?"

"The criminal. He went into his father's room and brought out the handle of an axe."

"Really?" Bola exclaimed, alarmed.

"At the sight of this everyone ran away. I closed my door, but watched everything through the window. The boy rushed at Mr Egbor, but his mother was in the way. He pushed past her, and came outside. At this time Mr Egbor himself had taken shelter in a room next door. The boy's madness became doubled when he did not see either Paul or his father. He was shouting that they should come out. But nobody came out to him."

"Who would come out to a madman?" the woman who lived in the room and parlour opposite said. She had come to join our crowd when she knew what we were talking about.

"So you too were in here at the time, madam?" I asked her. Her face looked familiar. But I did not know she lived in the house.

"I was in, sir. But I locked my door. I watched everything through my window."

"Did you know that the mad boy smashed the windscreen of Mr Abiola's car?" Mr Nwanna said. "He was annoyed that he had found neither Paul nor his father."

"Really?" Bola asked, excited.

"The car was parked right here," he indicated the spot outside the house. By this time more people had joined us. Nwanna continued his story.

"After he'd damaged the car he was going back to the house. But his mother held on to his trousers, pleading with him not to commit murder. The foolish boy pushed his mother away angrily. But she followed him, and held to his shirt. Then Mr Egbor came out, trying to get the axe handle from him. The boy tried to hit Mr Egbor with it. But swinging the axe handle back before hitting Mr Egbor, it hit his mother on the head, and she fell down."

"That was when Elizabeth shouted that Gilbert had killed his own mother," Mrs Palmer said. She was the woman who occupied the room and parlour opposite Nwanna. She had again joined in the narrative. "I was frightened. Real frightened. I refused to open my door and my window. That boy is mad sir, that boy they call Gilbert."

"It sounds like it," I said.

"The boy is a killer," Nwanna told us. "His mother stirred on the floor after some time and she wailed faintly: 'Gilbert has killed me. Oh, Gilbert has killed me.' She rolled from side to side. I was watching everything from my window."

"I, too, heard her saying that," Mrs Palmer confirmed. "But I refused to come out. I was frightened, I cannot deceive you. Who wants to be butchered by a madman? Everyone knows that the boy lives on Indian hemp. I kept my door locked," she laughed.

"And where's the woman now, Mr Nwanna?" I asked.

"In hospital, sir."

"And Jonathan? Where's he?"

"I hear he's gone to look for his wife and children. The wife was frightened. She has run away with the children. I think they will soon be back."

However, when we got home that night a friend of Jonathan's was waiting for us. I asked him where Jonathan was. He gave us bad news. The woman who was being treated in hospital for injuries received during the affray at 22 Fasanya Street had died. Both Jonathan and his son Paul, another woman living in the house, her daughter, and Gilbert, the son of the deceased woman, had all been locked up at the police station for their part in the murder of the deceased woman.

We were back where we started. Jonathan was, in truth, in trouble. He was in police custody.

THREE

Raliatu came at dawn the following morning, full of tears. She was completely void of ideas, positive or negative. Incoherently she told her story, punctuating it with sobs.

Apparently, on that fateful afternoon, she had gone to the primary school nearby where she sold rice to children who attended the afternoon session. On her return late in the evening, she had found that only one of her daughters was at home. This child had told her what she, herself, had been told. There had been a big fight in the compound which had involved her father, her brother, and some of the co-tenants in the house. Raliatu's daughter had told her that she had been told that one of the women had been wounded and had been taken to the hospital. The daughter had also told her that her husband had gone to the police station. They had had to leave the house at once because Raliatu had been afraid that the co-tenants in the house would harm her and her children. When she had not seen her husband back from the police station that night, she had concluded that the police had arrested him, and so she had sent her daughter Alice to my house to let me know what had happened, in the belief that I could persuade the police to release her husband.

Raliatu said Jonathan had come back from the police station late at night and the following morning had traced her and her children to the relative's place at Mushin where they were staying. She had, however, been advised not to follow her husband back to 22 Fasanya Street yet, but to allow tempers to cool first. Now, however, instead of tempers cooling down and things returning to normal, the woman who was wounded in the fight and who was receiving treatment in hospital had died, and her husband had been arrested by the police.

"You know there's something I've not told you yet," Bola said guiltily as we sat at breakfast, after Raliatu had told her story and I had told her to wait in the kitchen while Bola and I considered how to take the next step in what had once again become a serious matter.

"Yes?"

"Raliatu knew that there was going to be trouble," she said.

"She did?"

"Yes. Someone told her."

"Who?"

"One Malam."

"A Malam. Not an Aladura this time," I said sarcastically.

Bola knew that I do not have faith in prophets and prophetesses. She knew that I thought little of Malams, and less still of Babalawos.

"No, a Malam. Not an Aladura. She came to tell me the story about six weeks ago. Maybe a little earlier. I don't quite remember now."

"Sugar please—I'm sorry to interrupt your story," I apologized.

"That's sugar right in front of you, Daddy," Bola said, pointing to the sugar bowl right under my nose. I apologized for my absent-mindedness and asked her to proceed with the prophecy story.

"The Malam told Raliatu that there was going to be big trouble for her, and that she should slaughter a goat in sacrifice."

"The usual story. Besides, it is the husband now in trouble, not Raliatu," I commented, showing my disbelief in such nonsense.

"And is the husband's trouble not her trouble?" she asked.

"Presumably they sacrificed the goat?" I was curious to know.

"Yes, and no."

"What do you mean by yes and no?"

"Jonathan refused to give Raliatu the money for the goat."

"Wise man," I said, in praise of the absent Jonathan. He had done precisely what I would have done in his position.

"But Raliatu bought a goat all the same. From her housekeeping money."

"Wise woman. So long as she fed her husband and her family round the month. But is it in spite of the goat sacrifice that Jonathan is still in trouble? I think the Malam has read his prophecy upside down," I commented.

"What you don't know is that Jonathan's trouble could have been more serious than what it is now if Raliatu hadn't slaughtered the goat," Bola pointed out.

"A charge of manslaughter! Could even be murder, we don't know yet," I remarked. "Could anything be more serious than that?"

"Manslaughter?" she asked, alarmed.

"Or murder," I confirmed. "It could well be murder."

"That would be serious, Daddy."

"Very serious. Still, let's hear what the lawyer boys will say."

It took me a long time getting to the office that morning. The traffic congestion was particularly bad and was made worse by a number of vehicles that had broken down. There were two cases of vehicles changing flat tyres on the highway. There were two cases of vehicles in collision. None of them would move till the police came to take measurements and do a sketch for a report, which was a requirement for making a claim on the insurance company.

I have always wondered how much the nation lost in the colossal number of man-hours that are wasted in these traffic hold-ups. What, of course, would be difficult to assess is what the nation lost in the incidence of hypertension resulting from the bad temper and anxiety in the individual that is caught in the hold-up.

Belo's telephone worked, thank God. He was my lawyer friend. I explained to him Jonathan's trouble and asked what the prospect was.

"Bad, I'm afraid. Very bad. Did you say one of the people involved in the affray has died?" he asked.

"Yes, that's what we were told this morning."

"Quite bad, Kola," he repeated. "Your man is likely to be charged with manslaughter. Your blessed police might even charge him with murder."

"I am listening."

"Whatever the charge, though, he is nearly certain to get away."

"Yes?"

"Oh, yes. Unless, of course, he truly did the woman in. Which doesn't sound like the case from what I hear you say of your man Jonathan."

"All the evidence is that the woman died from a blow struck by mistake by her own son."

"If there are no complications, I think your man will get away. Normally there would be no doubt about his being set free. The real trouble is how long it takes to get the case to court and how long it lasts. You know the terrible congestion in the courts now."

"How do I arrange bail for him?" I asked.

"Through your lawyer, of course. But I suspect the police won't allow bail while the investigation lasts, and that could be a long time. You know what the police are. They go about the whole thing in a very clumsy manner. And by the way, you should not be in a hurry to ask for bail, particularly for a manslaughter charge. Someone accused of murder will not be given bail."

"You seriously think he might be charged with murder?" I asked, anxiously.

"I don't know. But you never know what the police and..."

"Hello, hello, hello...?" I cried into the receiver. The telephone had gone dead.

"Hello, hello, hello?" I shouted. There was no response. I dialled the number again. It was engaged. Five minutes later I dialled it again. Again it was engaged. And when I dialled it after another fifteen minutes, it was still engaged. I cursed the P & T.

After attending to some papers that had accumulated on my desk, I went to the First Mainland Police Station to find Jonathan. I had trouble finding a place to park my car. Everywhere was marked "no parking." This meant that I had to park a considerable distance away and walk back to the station.

"Can I watch your car?" a thin voice said behind me as I started to walk towards the police station. I turned round to confront a little urchin in a singlet and blue jeans. I wondered why he was not at school. I asked him why.

"I go to afternoon school," he said. "Can I watch your car?"

If I denied his request, he might steal the wheel covers, which were the most easily removable of the car's accessories. Such little urchins are the worst thieves. However, give them 10 kobo or even 5 kobo and they will stand guard over your car and keep others of their kind away. I gave him a 10k piece and told him to watch my car.

I picked my way through the crowd which milled round the desk sergeant at the police station. There was a bald-headed man in a French suit who appeared to be quarrelling with the police officer.

"Look, officer, I just have to have someone to follow me to the place now," the man said, beating his fist on the desk. "I must have a policeman to witness what the man is doing there."

"But Oga, I've told you that I cannot leave the station. I must not leave the station. I'm the only one here," the police officer insisted.

"So what should I do then? Someone has to come with me. Right now. Some officer of the peace must come to see what my landlord is doing."

"See my trouble now," the policeman said in despair, putting down the pen with which he had been taking down the statement of some other citizen. "I've told this Oga to report to the Assistant Superintendent of Police. ASP can arrange for some other officer..."

"But your ASP is not on seat. Not on seat, d'you hear. So, what do I do?"

"Look Oga, I must not leave the station. I beg you. If you want to make a statement, I give you the form. But..."

"No, someone has to come and see what my landlord is doing right now," the bald-headed man insisted. "Making a statement will not help me."

"But Oga. All these other people want me. You want me. Am I to divide myself into two? Am I to kill myself for government work? Am I?"

"Don't kill yourself," I said. "You are more useful to us alive than dead."

"But Oga, this other Oga wants me to kill myself. That's what he wants."

Seeing that I had diverted the attention of the desk sergeant from the citizen who wanted to take him away from his desk, I said: "I don't want you to come with me. What I want is information about someone I understand is in police custody here."

"What's the man's name?"

"Jonathan Egbor."

"Jonathan Egbor. Are you sure he's detained in this station?"

"No, I'm not. But I'm told he's here."

"Is it a case of two fighting?" he asked.

"Fighting, yes. But the number is probably more than two," I said.

"Where did the people fight? Which address?"

"Fasanya Street."

"Fasanya Street, Fasanya Street," he repeated the address, looking at me. "But why do you come here if the people fought at Fasanya Street?"

"I am told the man is detained here," I said.

"If the fight took place at Fasanya Street, then you go to Mainland Police Station No 2. Fasanya Street is under the jurisdiction of No 2, Oga."

At Mainland Police Station No 2, Jonathan Egbor's name and that of his son Paul Egbor were on the register of persons in cells under police investigation. The officer in charge of the investigation was out on another assignment. When I asked when he was expected to come back, I was told that it might be one hour, might be two, might be three. No one could say exactly. If I liked I could wait. Otherwise, I could come back the next day. I asked if there wasn't someone else who could give me permission to see Jonathan Egbor for a brief moment. I was told no. I was told that not even a senior officer could give me permission. In any case, I was told, the ASP was not on seat.

That night I ran into M.A. Natural at the City Club. His real name was Martin Abiola, but we all called him M.A. Natural, that is, a Master of Arts acquired naturally as opposed to one obtained in a university. He enjoyed the nickname because it suggested that he was a learned man.

"I hear you had a misadventure with your car the other day," I teased him.

36

"That was a serious matter and you are mentioning it lightly," he said, bending over the billiards table, ready for a stroke. He steadied himself carefully. He took a last look at the positions of the red and his opponents' white balls. Then very gently, very carefully, he slid the cue forward.

"Six," I shouted excitedly.

"Good stroke," his opponent conceded.

"Thank you," M.A. Natural said, as the cue boy brought the red ball back to position and M.A. again prepared for the next stroke. This time he made an easy two off the red. He again prepared for another stroke. Carefully, carefully. But to everyone's surprise, he missed completely, conceding an easy point to his opponent.

"You know that's your fault, Kola," M.A. Natural said.

"Why?" I asked.

"That matter you raised disturbed my concentration."

"But you scored a six and a two."

"It was a serious matter you raised, man. I tell you that boy was a raving maniac."

"I understand everyone ran away from him."

"My turn? Wait," he said, studying the configuration of the three balls on the table. After some time he bent down, took a careful aim, and struck his ball. He scored nothing this time. "Yes, everyone ran away. But Sissy Bintu and I watched him through the window."

Sissy Bintu was the pet name for Mrs Palmer, M.A. Natural's girlfriend at 22 Fasanya Street.

"Yes, she told me that."

"When he smashed my windscreen, I shouted."

"You did?"

"You know my first thought was to run out to confront the wretch. But Sissy Bintu stopped me. That boy could have killed me. He could have killed anyone."

"I hear he really could have killed Jonathan if that one had waited."

"I'm sure he could. The boy just went wild. How he pushed his mother so violently. It was the axe handle that he..."

"When you two have finished your story, call me," M.A. Natural's opponent said, taking a long draught from his glass of stout. He had gone to sit on one of the chairs along the wall.

"Oh, I'm sorry," M.A. Natural hurried back to the billiard table. Again he studied the field. He made a break of thirteen in five strokes. He came back to me and continued the story: "If you saw the way the maniac wielded the axe handle. He hit his own mother with it. That poor woman just slumped under the blow and passed out. In fact, everyone thought that she had died. She was later taken to the hospital in a taxi."

"Have you heard that the woman has in fact died now?"

"You don't mean it," he shouted, surprised.

"She died in hospital yesterday."

"Are you serious?" he asked with anxiety.

"Hasn't Mrs Palmer told you?"

"No. I haven't seen her since that time. If it is true that that woman has died, then that boy has killed his own mother," he said, slowly. "The boy should be held for manslaughter. And that is a serious matter. Very serious matter, I tell you."

"The boy is already in custody," I said. "But unfortunately, Jonathan Egbor, his son, and two women are also in a police cell now."

"Really? But that man Jonathan Egbor was only separating them. Man, that maniac was the killer," he declared, going back to the billiard table.

FOUR

The police struck at 22 Fasanya Street at dawn the following day. Gregory, the relation of Jonathan who lived not far from the place, brought the story to us later that evening. Apparently, the timing of the raid was to ensure maximum catch for the police net. And from the results, it could not have been better. A few of the men residents at No. 22 were already up, ready for the long trek to the factories at Ikeja or the shorter trek to the bus stages for the early ride to Lagos and Apapa. It was the only way they could avoid the rush which started forming at the bus stops by seven. There was a scuffle between a few of the residents and the police before they were forced into a police Land Rover. Most of the other residents at No. 22 were still in their cover cloths and pyjamas. A number of those who would not willingly go into the police vehicles were roughly handled.

As Gregory told the story, I saw a clear picture of the men and women of No. 22 scrambling like rabbits out of the twenty-four holes in which they lived on both the ground floor and the top floor, and getting in the way of one another in an attempt to escape the police.

"But why was it necessary to do it this way? Why was it necessary to terrorize respectable, law-abiding citizens at that infernal hour of the day?" I asked Belo, my lawyer friend, when I related the story to him later.

"Respectable, yes," Belo said slowly. "Law-abiding, yes and no. In any case, man, ours has not been a law-abiding society since you and I became adults."

"Yes? So?"

"The police action at Fasanya Street yesterday is an over-reaction to an ever-deteriorating state of affairs, the escalating wave of violence in our society, and the continuously diminishing resources of the police to cope with the situation. It makes them touchy."

I nodded. I was trying hard to follow him.

"I'm glad you see what I am trying to point out," Belo said, dropping the stub of his cigarette and crushing it under his left shoe. "You see, what the police do here in this country is just not done in any civilized society. Here the police justify their brutality and clumsiness by blaming them on the unfortunate attitude of our society, one which refuses to co-operate with the police in apprehending offenders and bringing them to book."

"I understand all that," I said. "But do they have to do things that frighten people away from them?"

"No, they don't have to."

"By the way, I haven't told you that they came to me, too," I said.

"They did? Were they rough with you, as well?" Belo asked, stroking his beard and smiling in a cross between mischief and anxiety.

"Someone came to me in the office. A young man who appeared bright and intelligent. Apparently, he had first called at the house before coming to the office."

"What did he want?"

"A statement. Said the police were investigating the affray at 22 Fasanya Street, and contacting everyone who might be able to help them. I told him I couldn't give him any statement. I was not at Fasanya Street when the event occurred and did not see why he had come to me."

"And what did he say then?"

"He said he had been sent by his superior officer to contact me as they had gathered from the statement of one of the persons under investigation that I might be able to testify to the character of one of the accused. Something to that effect. I told him I could certainly testify any day to the character of Jonathan Egbor, who he confirmed was detained by the police. But I was not at Fasanya Street and so..."

"You could not and should not make any statement. That's that. You were quite right. You don't have to testify to the character of Jonathan Egbor either. At least not till he has been found guilty and the judge requires evidence that he was not a seasoned criminal and all that. We've not reached that stage; not yet."

In all this time, we still had not seen Jonathan. I had tried thrice and Bola once. But we just hadn't been lucky. In her case, she met an over-zealous senior officer who refused to allow her to contact a person in police custody in the absence of proof of very close relationship with that accused person. In my case, the officer investigating the case had been out each time I had called. And each time I had called, the superior officer in charge of the whole station had not been on seat either.

"Not on seat"—the classical bastard offspring of culpable malingering and the inevitable consequence of a poor telephone service. For if each time that I had left my own desk to go to the police station someone had called wanting to see me in my office, I too would certainly be labelled "not on seat." And someone calling in that person's own office at that same time would also find him "not on seat." Yet these absences from one's desk would have been absolutely unnecessary if the telephone service had been reliable.

The first feedback about the result of the police raid at 22 Fasanya Street came four days after the raid when I had four visitors late at night. As usual, NEPA, the National Electric Power Authority that held the monopoly for the supply of electricity in the country, had "taken away" the light. Inside the sitting-room was hot. So Bola and I were sitting in the verandah after we had put the children to bed. We were doing our best, in spite of the mosquitoes, to enjoy the welcome light from a quarter moon.

I recognized Gregory but not the others. They introduced themselves as members of the Esala Progressive Union, Lagos Branch, and friends and relations of Jonathan Egbor on his father's side. They had come to see me in both capacities to thank me and my wife for all that we had been doing for Jonathan since he was a boy, since I got him trained both as a mechanic and driver, and later got him a good job in the Housing Authority. They thanked me for the part my wife and I played in helping him get a wife when he was old enough to take one, and for organizing the dowry paid on Raliatu. They catalogued all these things to the point of embarrassing us.

In particular, they had come now to thank us for all we had been doing to help Jonathan and his wife Raliatu since the trouble started a few days before. They wanted us to know that they, the members of the Esala Progressive Union, had not been inactive since the unfortunate incident. They had been running about. Very much, too.

They had now confirmed what they had suspected since the woman involved in the affray had died in the hospital: that the trouble Jonathan Egbor was in was very serious indeed. The raid on 22 Fasanya Street and the way the police treated the victims of the raid at the police station also confirmed that. They knew that what had happened would require seeing the police. Not at the police station. Not in the open. But in the way those unfortunate enough to fall into the net of the police usually see them.

They told me that they knew I could not understand or agree with them as to the way they were organizing going about the matter. But they were certain that otherwise Jonathan Egbor and his son Paul would go to gaol. They wanted me to continue to play my part at the high level at which they knew I was competent. I should leave them to play their part at the level where they had the greatest competence. The level at which they and the police spoke a common language. From the dawn raid at Fasanya Street, they had seen that each one of them now had to work hard and play the game the police way.

I took the hint that I must not allow the police to identify me with Jonathan's case, otherwise I might prejudice whatever chances of success they might have with their method of dealing with the police. It might well achieve success, judging from the stories one usually heard of the goings-on in matters like this. All the same, I had to see Jonathan. And as he was still held by the police, I had to look for him at the police station.

Eventually, I made it. It was on a day and at a time that the Police Inspector investigating the case was "on seat." He confirmed that Jonathan Egbor and three others connected with the 22 Fasanya Street affray were in police cell 2. Yes, I could see them, but he did not have the competence to grant such permission, he told me politely. For this, I had to see his superior officer. And double luck; that worthy too was "on seat." But I had to wait a little as there was someone with him in his room.

I did not have very long to wait. The superior officer came, followed by an Alhaja with all the regalia of her class—an iro and buba of an expensive cream lace, with the characteristic double-tier headgear. She wore expensive jewellery, the type that was imported from Beirut and smuggled through the customs at Ikeja. These Alhajas! They had cause to keep close to the police and the customs people.

As the police boss passed me, I thought I recognized him. He himself looked back and stopped. Yes, I certainly knew him. "Mr. Banjo?" he inquired.

"Yes. Dada—ASP Dada?" I returned his question.

"Glad to see you, sir," he said, moving back to me. The Alhaja moved back with him. "Why, I haven't seen you since, since 1943."

That was true. That was the year I left Ibadan State College as head prefect. He was in Form III then, a particularly bad boy. "How are you, sir?"

"I'm very well," I told him. "Won't you finish attending to Alhaja first?" I suggested gallantly.

"Oh, that's alright. She will not mind," he said, looking at her with an eye suggestive of extra-mural desires.

"I don't mind, sir," Alhaja said in a strangely manly voice completely out of place in a female, particularly an Alhaja of her charms. "But I want you, sir, to help me beg ASP to help me beg the Inspector to help me."

"Do help Alhaja, Mr. Dada," I interceded on her behalf.

"Oh, Alhaja? She's alright. She can wait," Dada said, leading the way back to his room. There we exchanged a few reminiscences of our school days at State. He was a lazy, untidy boy and I remembered how I had, on one occasion, reported him to be caned for being the ringleader of a group of boys who had broken bounds to enjoy themselves at a disreputable bar in town instead of going to work on their agricultural farms.

Eventually, he wanted to know what had brought me there, and I told him.

"I think I've heard of the case. And the boys are still investigating," he told me. "Actually, the officer in charge of the case does not belong to this branch. He comes from the homicide branch. Sergeant?" he shouted through the half-open door.

The desk sergeant came in and saluted smartly.

"Sergeant, find out for me if the homicide officer investigating the case of the murder at... what's the street now?"

"Fasanya Street," I helped him.

"Find out if he's there. Tell him I want to see him."

"Yes, sir."

I confirmed to him that the officer was in, as I had just spoken to him before coming to see the ASP.

"Tell him I want to see him right now," ASP Dada repeated his instruction.

"Yes, sir," the sergeant said, again saluting smartly before departing. A few minutes later he came back with the officer investigating the case. Both of them saluted.

"Ah, sergeant?"

"Yes, sir."

"You know this Oga here?"

"No, sir," the man lied. I had introduced myself to him only minutes before.

"He's the biggest Oga in the Lagos State Housing Authority," ASP Dada too lied. I was No. 2 in my own department of the Authority and only No. 4 in the whole hierarchy.

"Yes, sir."

"He wants to see one of the men in cell. I hope that's alright?"

"Yes, sir."

"What's the name of your man, sir?" he turned to me.

"Jonathan Egbor."

"Jonathan Egbor. You hear, sergeant?"

"Yes, sir."

"Wait, sergeant," ASP Dada said in an apparent afterthought.

"Yes, sir?" the junior officer wheeled round.

"I think you should bring the man here. Not a violent case, I hope?"

"No, sir."

"No security problem? Then bring him here. I think it's more convenient that you should see him here," he told me after the sergeant had left. "You won't have a chance to hear what you are saying in that place. About ten people in the cell. Part of the problem we are combating in the force."

"You must have many problems, I'm sure," I commented.

"Plenty, sir. No money for building new stations. No money for buying new vans for transporting officers to accident scenes and crime scenes. No money to pay police informers. Not sufficient hands..."

"It must be very hard for you."

"It is very hard for us, sir. Very frustrating. And the public don't appreciate our problems... Yes, come in."

The sergeant came in, followed by Jonathan Egbor.

"Master, master," Jonathan cried.

"Jonathan?"

"Master, they say I killed that woman," he cried. "How can I kill the woman when..."

"Keep cool, Jonathan," I advised. I suppressed my feeling of horror at how emaciated he had become in the few days in which he had been in police custody. Presumably, every day in that inhospitable cell was like a year in the free, though overcrowded environment, of Fasanya Street.

"Master, how could I have killed the woman?" Jonathan repeated. "I was the one separating them. And everyone knew that the woman died of the wound which her son gave her."

"Keep cool, Jonathan," I counselled again as his voice rose in proportion to his rising emotion.

"Master, how could I have killed her and then run to the police station here to report the fight? How is that possible?" I was certain he did not kill the woman, nor contribute to her death. But I saw at once that his line of argument would not impress the judge if he was dragged to court for murder or for manslaughter.

"But where's Paul?" I asked.

"He's there, master. He's in the cell," Jonathan answered, shrugging his shoulders.

"Are there two of them?" ASP Dada asked the officer in charge of the investigation.

"No, sir. Five of them, sir."

"Five?" ASP Dada said, surprised, looking at me. "Mr. Banjo, you know these others?"

"No, I know only Jonathan Egbor and Paul Egbor. They are father and son."

"Father and son! Father and son took part in the same fight?" the ASP asked the investigating officer.

"Yes, sir."

"But I never fight. I never fight, sir," Jonathan wailed. "Master, it was that mad boy Gilbert that was fighting Paul. And I was only separating them. Master, master..." and here Jonathan broke down. He sobbed uncontrollably.

I was sad, very sad, when ASP Dada told me that there was little I could do to help Jonathan and Paul at that stage. Since someone had died as a result of the affray, all persons known to have taken part in the affray just had to be kept in custody while police investigation lasted.

FIVE

A few days later we had information that alarmed us. The statements made to the police by Jonathan's co-tenants at Fasanya Street were most damaging to Jonathan's case. A number of the men had said that they were away from home when the fighting took place and that they had only been told about it by their wives and children. Those of the women who confirmed that they were in when the fighting took place said that they saw nobody hit anybody. A number of them had said that they saw nothing and heard nothing. One woman, however, a relation of the woman that died, said that she saw Jonathan hit the deceased woman with an axe. Gilbert Bassey, the son of the deceased woman, also said that Jonathan hit his mother with a piece of iron and kicked her in the tummy till she fell. No one had said that he had seen Gilbert Bassey hold any dangerous weapon or that he had injured his mother, nor that she had fallen, hitting her head during the fall.

The implication was obvious. If two people in their statements said that Jonathan hit the dead woman with a dangerous weapon, and if no one said in his statement that he saw Gilbert Bassey wield a dangerous weapon or saw him hit his mother, though unintentionally, and that she fell and knocked her head on the floor—in these circumstances the hangman's noose, originally hanging only loosely round Jonathan's neck, was now obviously pulled tighter. That Jonathan might be hanged for a murder that he did not commit had up till now only been a remote possibility. But now it was no longer so very remote.

"It is the problem we face all the time," ASP Dada said seriously when I told him in his office what I had heard. "This is the trouble we have with the public. Nobody is willing to come forward to tell the police what he knows."

"So I see. But what's the explanation?"

"They say they are afraid of the police. Why they are afraid of the police I don't know. You hear this funny story, sir," he said, chuckling and relaxing in his chair. "My own mother told me this story when I went home last week. She told me of a motor accident that occurred near her stall at the market. She said she saw a tipper carrying sand collide with a taxi, pushing the taxi into the ditch. She said they all ran helter-skelter and deserted the market for the rest of the day."

"They deserted the market?"

"Oga, they all ran away for the rest of the day. But the interesting thing is this: my mother told me that when the motor traffic unit people came to investigate the accident the following day, a number of the market women again ran away. But my mother did not run away."

"Presumably, being the mother of a police superintendent, she would know that there was nothing to fear from the police."

"But you know what happened next?"

"What happened?"

"When the police corporal went to my mother's stall and asked if she saw the accident, she said that she had not seen the accident at all! She said it was true she was at the stall, but she was asleep!"

"Really?"

"Most of the other women in fact said that they were away from the place when the accident occurred. Now tell me, what can you do with people like that? Just what can you do with them?"

"But why are they so afraid of the police?"

"Something to do with what the public regard as wasting time... the repeated visits to the police station that investigation involves." He had explained what I already knew.

"And presumably the possibility of having to go to court to give evidence. That is truly enough to discourage anyone from wanting to come forward to help the police with any information, in view of the endless adjournments in every court case."

It was not all the men at 22 Fasanya Street who had made statements to the police. One man, Emmanuel Ojerinde, had run away the day news of the death of Marian Bassey filtered back to the other tenants at that address. Another man had sent his wife back to their home town beyond Akure.

When I told Alex Belo, my lawyer friend, about the latest development, he confirmed that the situation was bad but by no means as desperate as I had thought. He was certain that my man Jonathan would not hang unless, of course, he truly committed the crime. Even then, it would be difficult to prove conclusively that he did. And no court would convict an accused person of murder unless the prosecution completely proved the person's guilt beyond reasonable doubt. The onus of proof of guilt lay with the prosecution more than the onus of proof of innocence lay with the accused person. All the same, we must find one or two people who could testify that they did not see Jonathan or his son hold an offensive weapon or push the woman that died. They must also testify that they, in fact, saw someone else commit the crime. Unless, of course, our man and his people had not been telling the truth.

"But how now can we find people to testify on our side?" I asked him. We were both in my office.

"What about the man you say has run away?" he asked.

"Yes, what about him? He has already run away."

"Then we've got to find him."

"Find him? How do we find him?" I asked.

"I don't know. And I don't think you can know. But man, doesn't your man Jonathan have people? Just what are they doing in all this?"

"You mean they can find him?"

"They can. And they must, if their man is not to swing on the hangman's rope."

We were both silent for some time. Then I saw the snag. "But even if Jonathan's people succeed in locating the man that ran away, why should we think he will want to come back and give evidence for us? Remember he ran away in the first instance precisely because he did not want to get involved with the police."

We both looked towards the door. A clerk came in with a file. I was a bit cross that he had come in to disturb an important dialogue. But then I had not told anyone that I was not to be disturbed. We both watched him put the file in the in-tray, extract another one from the middle of the pending-tray, and then walk out.

"You saw the point I made?" I asked Belo.

"Yes, of course. But as I was about to say, we have to get that man, and get him to come and give evidence for us."

"Just how do we do that? That's what I'd like to know," I asked.

"Jonathan's men will know what to do. They'll know how to find him. And how to get him to come and give evidence. You will be useless in this aspect of the case."

"Quite."

"But, but..." he looked at me as if he'd suddenly struck a new idea.

"Yes, what is it?"

"Didn't you tell me that M.A. Natural was there on the day of the fight?" he asked, looking at me with curiosity and mischief lighting his face. The reference was to Martin Abiola.

"Yes, he was."

"I suppose he hasn't made any statement to the police?"

"No, he hasn't. He couldn't."

"I suppose his wife mustn't know that he was visiting—who's the woman now?"

"Mrs. Palmer. Sissy Bintu. That's the girlfriend."

"And the wife mustn't know that he was at Fasanya Street. I see. I see," Belo said, nodding his head.

"I wonder what he told his wife about the damage to his Toyota Crown," I said.

"Oh, that was damaged?"

"The maniac smashed the windscreen."

"Really? Interesting!"

"Presumably he would invent a good story. I would in the same circumstances," I said, laughing.

"You know something, Kola? We must get M.A. Natural to give evidence. And we must get his girlfriend to give evidence too."

"Mrs. Palmer? She has said in her statement that she saw nothing—absolutely nothing."

Then, of course, there was Nwanna, the man who occupied the first of the two front flats on the ground floor. No one had told me what kind of statement he had made to the police. But I was certain he, too, must have followed the others. They had seen nothing. They had heard nothing. Absolutely nothing. I called at 22 Fasanya Street twice after this revelation about the type of statement that the residents had made about the fight. Both times Nwanna was out. So was Mrs. Palmer.

When next I called to see Jonathan at the police station, I took his wife Raliatu and one of his daughters with me. The police officer investigating the case was out on another assignment, but my friend ASP Dada was in, and he allowed me to see Jonathan. And as before, he was brought to the ASP's room, together with his son Paul.

"Master, I hear they all have told lies that they did not see Gilbert hold the axe handle," Jonathan said excitedly, cutting out the normal exchange of greetings. "Master..."

"Keep cool, Jonathan," I said, waving him to a stool at the corner.

"Let me stand like this, master. Those people at Fasanya Street master, they know the truth. But they are all telling lies now."

"I know they know the truth," I confirmed. "But Jonathan, we have to be cool about it."

"Yes, master. But those people want government to kill me. Don't they know that if they don't tell the truth now, government will believe I caused the woman's death and then kill me? And kill Paul too. That's what they want government to do to me and my son."

"We'll see that the truth truly comes out, Jonathan," I said, though I myself did not know any other way of getting the truth to come out except through those cowardly co-tenants of

Jonathan's at 22 Fasanya. They would have to come out and rewrite their statements. All this time Paul said nothing.

Dada wanted to know if we had arranged a lawyer for Jonathan. I told him that Belo, my friend, was looking into the matter. "The lawyers know how to get the truth out of witnesses," he said. "Just wait till the case gets to court."

That was reassuring. But it would have been a lot more reassuring if people had come forward to tell the truth in the first instance instead of waiting till a bully of a lawyer forced the thing out of them in the witness box.

"But master, I beg you to get me out of this place quickly," Jonathan pleaded.

"But don't you see master is doing his best?" Dada asked, almost impatiently. "Master comes here to see you. Master is arranging a lawyer to defend you."

"But master, it is the suffering in this place that made me talk like that," Jonathan apologized. Paul still said nothing. He looked very sulky.

"That's alright, Jonathan. I'm sure we will soon get you out of here," I again reassured him. Of course, I had not the faintest idea of how we were going to do it.

"Raliatu has brought some food for you," I said, diverting his attention from his suffering.

"But master, I don't want food," Jonathan said in dejection.

"Look, Jonathan, you have got to eat," I bullied him. His daughter Alice started to cry. Paul now began to sob. So did Raliatu. "You will soon be out of this. And you've got to be a man," I said with an air of authority.

"Help me beg him to eat," Raliatu cried. "The food I brought yesterday, he did not eat a single morsel of it," she wailed.

"Don't you see you've got to eat?" I pleaded with him.

"But master, food is not important. I'm suffering in this place. Even the food Raliatu brought yesterday, did she not tell you what happened to it?" he asked, turning to Raliatu. We too turned to her.

"It was the other people with him in the cell," she sobbed, wiping tears off her face with her left hand.

"What about the other people with him in the cell?" I asked.

"They scrambled for the food. They were all eating it greedily. They did not even give Papa Paul a chance to eat a single morsel of it," she explained, still sobbing.

"Paul also did not eat?"

"I fought with them and got a little to eat," Paul said.

"How can I be struggling with those people for food?" Jonathan faced me. "Master, the suffering in this place is too much. I beg master to—take—me—a—way." He broke down.

"This is always happening," Dada confessed. "You know all sorts of people are in that cell. A number of them are ex-convicts. A number are Indian hemp smokers. And..."

"But why should they be kept with such people in the same cell?" I asked.

"They are all under investigation. That's the trouble. And besides, we are short of accommodation. Only two cells in the whole of this station. Government says there is no money. And yet they want an efficient police force."

"This is terrible," I said.

"It is terrible, sir. Everything in the police is terrible. No money. No men. No vehicles. I'm going to resign soon. I'm fed up," ASP Dada said.

"Government ought to do something about this. I'm sure they will," I consoled him with an assurance that both he and I knew had no foundation whatsoever.

"I'm going to do something now," Dada announced. "It is against regulations. But I accept responsibility for it."

"Yes?" I looked at him, wondering what the irregular thing was that he was going to do for which he was going to accept responsibility.

"Bring the food here," he ordered Raliatu.

She hurried to the corner where she had earlier placed a dish. She came back with it, removed the lid which she handed over to her daughter. It was rice with fish and pepper soup. I saw immediately that this was a richer meal than Raliatu would normally prepare for her husband back home at Fasanya Street. But then the circumstances were not normal. Her dear husband, Papa Paul, was suffering in police custody.

"Taste it," ASP Dada ordered.

I was surprised at the order. But I was more surprised still at the promptness with which Raliatu proceeded to sample the dish. Dada next took the spoon from her and proceeded to turn the contents of the dish from the bottom upwards. The operation reminded me of the dexterity with which labourers in a building operation mix cement, sand and gravel to produce concrete.

"Yes, that's alright," Dada said, passing the dish back to Raliatu for onward transmission to her husband and her son. "We have to do this," the police officer said in anticipation of my question. "We cannot afford to take chances with prisoners and men in police custody. First, their relatives could pass poison to them, through food."

"To kill them off?" I asked, astonished.

"Yes. Murder. Or suicide, if the poison was first extracted and later self-administered by the accused person," he said, drawing a fine line between the two.

"With the wife first eating some of the food, we are certain that she could not have poisoned it. You see what I mean?"

"I see," I said.

"Then what I did myself was to check if any implement was hidden in the food. You know there are cases on record where prisoners have sawn through prison bars with tiny hacksaws and similar little implements. You don't know what criminals and their collaborators can do, sir."

"I see," I repeated.

"Thank God the criminals and accused persons we deal with here are still unsophisticated. But how long they will remain so, we don't know."

SIX

Gilbert Bassey, the unemployed son of the woman who died in the hospital, together with the two women in custody, were released by the police after six days in the cells. That Gilbert was released was surprising news in itself. But what made it doubly surprising was the fact that Jonathan Egbor and his son Paul were not released. Here was the man who everyone said they saw wield the weapon that felled his deceased mother, though accidentally, being let off by the police. Yet they continued to hold two men who everyone knew ought not to be held responsible for the death of the woman. The ways of our national police were in all ways like the peace of God which passeth all understanding.

I had at one time toyed with the idea that Jonathan would be released by the police after they had established the fact that he was innocent and that he was only playing the part of a peacemaker in the affray. But I had since given up the hope of this since Belo warned me that in all likelihood the police would, in the first instance, prefer a charge of manslaughter against all the people in custody and pass on the responsibility for letting any of them off to the magistrate, or the judge. But now that the police had let off Gilbert Bassey, the man truly responsible for the death of his own mother, and had continued to hold Jonathan Egbor and his son Paul, I became quite concerned. Where now could one find justice?

As if that was not enough, the investigation of the case against these two was transferred away from Mainland Police Station No. 2 to the General CID Headquarters on the Island. And of course, the two men who were being investigated were themselves physically transferred to that fearful place. This time they were made to occupy two different cells, both quite forbidding.

There were a number of other people at that time being investigated by the police. It was bad enough trying to see Jonathan at the Mainland Police Station No. 2, but the terrible traffic congestion on the roads made motoring from Yaba to the Central CID Headquarters on the Island quite a serious undertaking.

The actual distance as recorded by the speedometer of my car on one occasion was a mere 15 kilometres. But by God, it sometimes took two hours, sometimes three, to do this relatively short distance. And it was not just the time taken that was the problem; there was also the toll on the car brakes and clutch.

A delegation of Jonathan's people again came to see me in my office to discuss the latest developments. They were bent on making the meeting more formal and elaborate than I wished. I was particularly busy that morning getting some statistics ready for the boss, which were to be embodied in another report for the Minister responsible for our Authority.

However, I had to see my visitors and hear what ideas they had because I was coming to the unhappy conclusion that it was these people, at their own level, who would eventually save Jonathan and Paul, if anyone could save them. They operated on a plane and wavelength not far from those of the police. Sadly, I was beginning to doubt my own capacity to save Jonathan and Paul, and to fear that the confidence Jonathan placed in me was not going to be justified. Indeed, I suspected that he was already coming to that conclusion himself because he thought that I held an exalted position which gave me an "open sesame" to all corridors of power and that I could just fix his release through a simple telephone conversation with the Commissioner of Police.

The spokesman for the delegation introduced himself as Isaiah Erebor, and said that he was a Senior Executive Officer in the Ministry of Trade. He was lean and looked undernourished. He introduced the delegation one by one, giving information that he considered important about each individual. This meant that he said more than was really necessary about everyone. He, for instance, said so much about the achievements and importance of Gregory Eregie that if I had not known him through Jonathan, I would have come to the conclusion that he was more important than he truly was.

"It is the chief masquerader that comes out last from the grove," Erebor said, pointing to the final member of the group. "This is why I have left the introduction of our father in Lagos to the last. The President of the Esala Progressive Union, Lagos Branch. A retired railway official with thirty-two years' service..."

"I'm pleased to meet you," I said, offering my hand. Erebor's method of introduction that had kept the old man's name to the last had become embarrassing. A man of double chieftaincy; Chief Joel Enobakhare," Erebor had at last landed with the vital information.

The old man shook my hand with genuine affection. He said the usual things—he had heard all the things that I had done for Jonathan. He had decided that he would follow his "children" that day to come to meet me and to thank me for all these things.

The telephone interrupted his expression of gratitude. "Yes? Yes? Who? No, I'm afraid there's no one of that name on this number. Who? What number did you want? Oh no, this is 4581, not 4851. Sorry, goodbye." It was a woman at the other end, which explained why I was not abrupt in cutting her off after I had discovered that she had the wrong number.

Pa Enobakhare emphasized that he and his union had come to the conclusion that the Jonathan case had escalated to a serious thing. "Palaver no de blow whistle, Oga," he announced, looking me in the face. "No special warning, no advertisement. Case done come for Jonathan Egbor. We all go fight case for Jonathan. He be one of our staunch members."

Then Isaiah Erebor took over from the President. He explained that they had decided to get a lawyer for Jonathan. He mentioned his name and said that he came from their town. They had not actually seen him to talk to because he was away on an overseas trip. But his wife had assured them that he was due back in another week.

"You see, my children argued much," Pa Enobakhare told me. "You see the amount of money we have with Treasurer—that one is for scholarship. So some people think say it is bad thing to spend scholarship money for court case."

I thought so too. But I refrained from saying so. I thought I would hear the old man out. I must be careful not to wound his sensibilities. Besides, I must be careful not to wade into Esala Progressive Union's domestic politics. So I allowed him to continue.

"But I say to my children: 'Palaver no de blow whistle.' So case has come. Which person fit get special money for house and yet suffer bad punishment for lack of money? So I tell my children. I tell them: let us get Jonathan Egbor out of trouble. Let scholarship wait. We who find money today for scholarship, we no fit find money again next year? Na so I tell them. They like talking grammar. Big grammar. But they do me the honour due to me. They know say I no go school proper and learn grammar. They agree we get Jonathan out of trouble. And we think we should tell you this."

"I'm glad to hear what you are doing," I said. "And I think Jonathan himself will be most thankful. All this would not have been necessary if only people had gone forward to speak the truth at the police station."

"No one can say the truth now that Mrs. Bassey died," Isaiah Erebor said.

"The police!" one man said. "Who wants to get into the clutches of the police? Bo, policeman not be good man, master. That's why no one wants to speak the truth."

"If I get brother for police, I go run from him," another said.

"And what beats me is why the police released that bad boy Gilbert Bassey," I said bitterly.

"That one, na money," Isaiah Erebor said.

"You mean the man whose wife died—Mr. Bassey went to give money to the police? No," I said in disbelief.

"Oga, I want tell you something," Pa Enobakhare said. "Listen to me. My people say when you shed tears for one eye, you keep the other eye free so you fit see the way you want go. You see wetin I mean?"

I nodded that I saw what he meant. In truth, I did not.

"Mr. Bassey. He done lose 'im wife. Now police catch 'im pickin..."

"You mean?"

"I mean say Bassey no want lose 'im pickin too," the old man declared.

When I told my lawyer friend Belo about the development, he expressed surprise. He said that the police releasing Gilbert Bassey did put a new complexion on the case. He wondered whether the police were truly satisfied that Gilbert Bassey was not responsible for the death of his mother and that Jonathan and his son Paul were more involved than we had been made to believe, or alternatively, the police might have decided to use Gilbert Bassey as a prosecution witness against Jonathan and Paul. He explained that the prosecution sometimes lets off one of the accused persons in a criminal case to use him in this role, which would make him freer to talk the truth against his former associates in crime.

"But why would the police want to use Gilbert Bassey against Jonathan and Paul, and not the other way round?" I asked Belo.

"I don't know really. One honestly doesn't know why our blessed police do half the things they do. Honestly," he said seriously.

As an afterthought he added: "Of course, the police may consider the story of a son killing his mother less credible than that of a man and his son causing the death of a woman co-tenant."

There was something in that supposition. Though it was obvious that whatever had made the police release Gilbert Bassey and hold on to Jonathan and Paul certainly made our case worse.

"What can we do now?" I said in despair.

"I wish I knew," Belo replied.

We both looked at each other for some time. We were in his office. I looked from him to the postcard-size photograph of his wife Ellen in an exquisite frame on his desk. Immediately the thought flashed through my mind that, in spite of this demonstration of loving attachment to Ellen, he had another woman who lived in a flat at Surulere. She already had two kids by him. And what was more, Ellen knew it.

"I wish I knew how to advise you in this matter, Kola," he said, bringing me back to the reality of the situation we were in. "This is a strange case. But I think we probably worry too much."

"Do you think so?"

"Yes I do. And, and... yes, who is it?" he said, lifting up the receiver of his intercom that had just rung. "No. I'm busy just now. Yes, I have someone with me. In another twenty minutes, perhaps. That's alright," he said, dropping the receiver.

After looking at me for a moment, he appeared to remember what he was saying before the intercom interrupted him. "You see, your man is still under investigation. No charge has been preferred against him."

"So?" I asked him.

"You cannot arrange a defence without a charge being preferred. That's the position in normal circumstances. Though I don't suppose you would consider these circumstances normal," he said, "and maybe we should be thinking of a defence lawyer."

"At least we should be making preliminary arrangements," I said. "Who would you suggest?"

"Oh, I don't know. I have to think. It comes back to the question of not knowing exactly what charges are being made. Look, leave this to me for a while."

Back in my office, I found Raliatu in my waiting-room. After reading a telegram in my in-tray and making a telephone call to the City Council in connection with the date of a meeting I was supposed to be having with the Deputy City

Engineer, I buzzed my secretary to ask Raliatu to come in.

"Did you see them last night?" I asked her without looking up from a file I had started reading. She sobbed in reply.

"What's the trouble now?" I looked at her. She was terribly distraught. "You've got to pull yourself together," I admonished her. "What do you get crying? Nothing. And why do you come to my office anyway? Why?"

"It's Papa Paul," she sobbed.

"Of course I know it's Papa Paul. And we are doing everything..."

"Master, please save me. Papa Paul is still refusing to eat," she sobbed more violently.

"Still refusing to eat?" I asked in alarm.

"Yes, master. He is wasting away. And he says—he says he wants to die. Master, please save me, please—save—me."

SEVEN

We got Jonathan eating again. It was the combined effect of Raliatu's tears, my wife Bola's persuasion, and my bullying that did it. Raliatu wanted to know from her husband what would become of her and her children if he should die and leave them alone in the harsh, hostile world. Bola reminded him that it was on occasions of stress like that that a man was known from a woman. If Jonathan behaved that way and resigned himself to fate at that stage, what would he expect a woman to do in similar circumstances?

I told him how silly it was to refuse food. If he continued to behave that way, I would wash my hands of his affair. He said he was sorry, and that he would himself want to live to prove that he had not committed the crime he had been accused of. He would like to live to shame those who had planned evil for him.

It was no more than a bold face I had put up when I was with Jonathan at the CID where he was detained. I had become more concerned and frightened by the new turn of events. Even though something told me that, however long it took, the truth would eventually come out and Jonathan would be set free, I also suspected that unless one or two of the people who saw the fight would come forward to tell the truth, then indeed Jonathan could be found guilty and hanged for murder.

The thought of it made me shudder. I was certain that Jonathan could not be convicted for murder, however, and that the worst that could happen to him was a conviction for manslaughter. Even without being a lawyer, I knew that you could not convict a man for murder unless you could prove what the legal people called malice aforethought. All the world knew, even the magistrate or the judge would know, the purity of Jonathan's heart. It was a heart that could not harbour any kind of malice, aforethought or afterthought.

I succeeded in tracking down Philip Nwanna at 22 Fasanya Street five days after Jonathan and Paul were taken to the Central CID. It was another one of those nights when NEPA had "taken away the light" from most places in Lagos. The illumination from the hurricane lantern on the top of the radiogram in Nwanna's sitting-room was not great. It was, however, enough for me to see from Nwanna's face that all was not well with him. When I asked him how he was, he confirmed that he had been ill.

"It's been bad all over the place," I said, taking my seat in one of the six chairs in the room. "It is this incessant rain. There's flu all over the place."

"I've been on sick leave for three days. And even the medicine the doctor prescribed I couldn't get in the hospital. After waiting in the queue for hours, they told me the medicine is not available."

"It must be terrible," I observed.

"Why does a doctor prescribe a medicine that he knows is not available in the hospital? I think the hospital staff have stolen the few medicines there to go and sell in their own private shops. Oga, terrible things are happening in this country."

"Yes, corruption is rampant. Everyone knows about it. The police, the doctors. All of them. Just what are the police doing in this matter?" I asked.

"The police!" he was derisive.

"You think they cannot do anything about it?"

"The police! What can they do? Is it not they and the hospital staff who steal the thing together? Let us talk something different, Oga."

It was my opportunity, and I seized it. "It's Jonathan Egbor's trouble," I said cautiously. "You hear the latest development?"

"Oga, I hear the police are still holding the man and his son. I wonder why they don't leave the poor man alone. He is innocent."

"You hear that they have now transferred them to the Central CID?"

"Is that so? These police people are terrible!"

I looked at him for a moment. I wasn't sure whether he truly did not know or he was only pretending not to know that Jonathan was at the Central CID.

"I saw him there yesterday. The police are really punishing the man and his son. And all this for a crime everybody knows they did not commit." I watched his reaction to this.

"You know our police. They can be ruthless. What they want is what they want. Money. And they will not leave Jonathan Egbor and Paul till they get plenty of money."

I waited for him to continue.

"Oga, I want to tell you something. If the father of a policeman is in trouble, his son—his own son—will first take money from him before he helps him. That's the police. I know them."

"But I hear that the case against Papa Paul is now serious because nobody among you people here told the truth about what happened during the fight. I hear that no one said that it was that woman's son who held the axe handle that accidentally wounded the mother."

Nwanna kept silent for a moment. I wondered if his silence indicated that my allegation—that not one of them, including him, had told the truth—had caused him embarrassment.

"You too have made a statement to the police, Mr. Nwanna?" I primed him.

"Oga, I have. And I could not tell the police that I saw anybody hold an axe handle," he confessed. He appeared angry and nervous.

"You could not?"

"I could not. Oga, this is big matter. Very big matter. And our police—they are terrible people. Very terrible people."

"Mr. Nwanna, I can understand your fear of the police, knowing them as we all do. But what is important is that with everyone being afraid of the police, no one is coming forward to tell the truth. That could lead to an innocent man being hanged for murder. That's what we must now consider."

Nwanna did not reply immediately. When he eventually spoke, he said: "Oga, that man, I mean Mr. Jonathan Egbor, he will be free. I am sure he will be free. And I pray for him every day that he will be set free. He and his son. Honest, I pray for both of them."

"We all are praying for them," I told him. "But prayer alone won't help Jonathan and Paul."

"But Oga, I cannot say in a statement to the police that I saw the man that held the thing that killed a person. To do that is to give a rope to the police to hang me. This is the truth of the matter, Oga."

"You can't say what is true even if it will help another man to get justice, Mr. Nwanna?"

"Oga, you want to know the truth?"

"Of course, I do!" I was getting waked up. So was he.

"You want to know the facts?" he again asked, this time adjusting his loin cloth round his waist.

"What are the facts, Mr. Nwanna?"

"They will kill me."

"They will kill you? Who?"

"They."

"Who are they? The police?"

"No, not the police."

"Who then?"

"They. The woman's people."

I looked at him in astonishment. I opened my mouth. I closed it, not sure of what to say that would be appropriate.

"Oga, I know what you may think of me. But if I say I know who held the axe handle, I will be killed. And I don't want to be killed."

He took a few steps to the lamp on the radiogram. He shook it to check if it needed more kerosene as the flame appeared to be diminishing in size. The operation of shaking the lamp improved the illumination. He put the lamp back and returned to his seat. And as he was taking his seat, "NEPA came back." The place suddenly became bathed in white light, the combined output of two forty-watt lamps on the wall.

"Good," I said, welcoming the diversion from rather tedious talk. But to my surprise, he himself went back to the matter in hand. "I pray for Jonathan Egbor. And I pray for his son Paul. I pray for both of them. And I know they will be free. This is all I can do now. If I do what you think I should do, they will kill me. Oga, they will kill me."

My attempt to introduce one or two items of non-controversial conversation to remove the rough edges from our embarrassing discussion did not achieve much. When I rose to go, both of us knew that the Jonathan Egbor case had come between us, putting a permanent strain on the otherwise good relationship.

Outside, I noticed that M.A. Natural was with Mrs. Palmer, alias Sissy Bintu. Whatever doubts I had previously entertained about the wisdom of calling to see her and appealing to her to make a new statement to the police—in which she would tell the truth about Gilbert wielding the weapon that had felled his mother—were now definitely resolved in favour of my not calling. At least not that night. She and M.A. Natural were in all likelihood in top gear in sex play at that moment. A call at that time would be a source of embarrassment and annoyance, and would very definitely not achieve the desired objective.

The tell-tale Toyota Crown was parked not outside 22 Fasanya but a few houses down the street. The unhappy events of that fateful night were still fresh in the minds of people, certainly in the mind of M.A. Natural who quite obviously did not want a repeat performance, which made him park his car away from No. 22. I walked down to have a closer look at the car. Of course, the windscreen had been replaced. Briscoe had certainly done a thorough job. They always did, damn their expensiveness. But which of the motor servicing places was not expensive? Even Mandilas that was once cheap was no longer the poor man's garage these days.

On my way home, I reflected sadly on my unhappy interview with Nwanna. Nwanna was afraid. Afraid not of the police, who were the usual subject of fear in cases like this. He was afraid of the relatives of the dead woman. Presumably, he was afraid of her husband and her son. Presumably afraid of a host of other relatives. And of the people from her village, beyond the extended family.

I knew, of course, that the fear of Marian Bassey's people only happened to be greater than his fear of the police. That latter fear was still there, very much alive too, even though submerged under the bigger fear of possible repercussions from the relatives of Marian Bassey.

The fear of the police! I remembered a story I had once heard. A woman had called at the police station to report that a child was missing. When asked where she had lost it, she had replied that it was, of all places, in a passenger minibus. Apparently, what had happened was that another woman, not the one who had come to make the report to the police but a relation, had alighted from the bus and had just forgotten to take the child out of the vehicle. Difficult to believe, but it happened. When eventually the actual woman who had behaved in this grossly careless manner turned up at the police station with a man she accused of being the driver of the vehicle and therefore the suspected child stealer, you would not believe how rough the police had been with all three of them. You would have thought that the women's emotional stress would have evoked sympathy and therefore gentle treatment from the police. Oh, no. Not at all. The suspected child stealer was in police custody for a whole week, while apparently the search for the missing child had continued.

What was more interesting, however, was what the police did when eventually another man turned up at the police station with the missing child. He explained that he was a minibus driver and that after he had made the last trip on a particular day and was on his way to the depot where he usually kept his vehicle, he heard the crying of a child in the passenger section of the bus. He stopped to find out what was happening. He discovered to his amazement a little child, without a mother. The child was too young to say who he was or where his parents lived. He took the child to his own home where he and his wife looked after him for a couple of days, during which time they hoped that the parents would come looking for the child. Eventually, he decided to take the child to the police station and explain what had happened. A rude shock awaited him at the police station. Instead of the police—who knew of a missing child and were holding a man in custody for the alleged theft of the child— thanking him for solving the mystery of the missing child, they treated him as if he was a criminal. There and then they clamped him in custody, in the company of the other man whose innocence had now been proved. And the two men were not released until they had appeared in the customary court for the offence of child stealing. Who would want to go willingly to the police in these circumstances?

My friend Belo was disappointed at the lack of success of my mission with Nwanna. He, however, insisted that we just had to persuade him to come forward to tell the truth.

"But how?" I asked.

"I don't know. But the man must be made to come forward," he said.

"He says the family will kill him if he comes forward."

"They might," Belo said, somewhat callously.

"But he doesn't want to be killed."

"I know. But he still must be made to come forward to tell the truth. He must. And what about M.A. Natural?"

"Yes, he too was at Fasanya Street last night."

"Was he?" Belo asked, his face lighting up with envy and a desire to break the Seventh Commandment. Subject: Sissy Bintu alias Mrs. Palmer. "And did you discuss the matter with them?"

"You mean the possibility of giving evidence for Jonathan Egbor?"

"Yes."

"I did not."

"No?"

"No. I did not."

"Why not, when you had the opportunity?"

"I think you are not being realistic, man," I said impatiently. "Nwanna said he's afraid of being killed. You admit that he well could be killed if he came forward to tell the truth. Yet you insist he must be made to come forward. How do we do it?"

"I don't know how. But he's got to be made to do it. Actually, it's Sissy Bintu and M.A. Natural I think you ought..."

"Listen, a man was in bed with his woman. You want me to open their bedroom door and start a discussion on the details of what happened the day some people fought outside their window?"

"Not realistic, I know. But still both Nwanna and M.A. Natural must be made to come forward to speak the truth. And what about the other man?"

"Which one?"

"The other one. Didn't you say another one ran away altogether?"

"Oh yes. I really..."

"They haven't found him?"

"Not until two days ago. When I saw Gregory the other day..."

"Who's Gregory?"

"Oh, one of them. Jonathan's people."

"If they haven't found him, they just have to find him. Man, they just have to. And people must be made to come forward to speak the truth. Honestly, no alternative, if our man is not to be convicted for murder."

"And be hanged?"

"Of course. He would be hanged if he was convicted of murder."

EIGHT

Emmanuel Ojerinde. That was the man who allegedly fled 22 Fasanya Street the day after Marian Bassey died in hospital. Ojerinde was obviously our man. We must get to him before the police did. If they found him before we did, they would muck him around to the point at which he too would say that he had seen nothing and had heard nothing. The story was that he had fled to his hometown, Ada, beyond Oshogbo. Jonathan's people were assigned the duty of reaching him there and persuading him to come back to Lagos to give evidence in our favour. Which should not be understood to mean that we were going to influence him in any way. That would be wrong. We were merely going to persuade him to come forward and speak the truth about the fight. Nothing more than that.

When Isaiah Erebor and three other members of the Esala Progressive Union called to see me at home one evening, I knew at once that they had drawn a blank. Who would think that a man who originally fled the city of Lagos and the particular trouble that it held for the residents of 22 Fasanya Street in connection with the death of Marian Bassey would willingly follow a number of people back to the same city to face the unpleasant music which originally made him run away? Why should anyone believe that Emmanuel Ojerinde would leave the security of his peaceful village and come back to Lagos? Jonathan's people had drawn a blank alright, but in a different way which none of us had bothered to consider. Emmanuel Ojerinde was not in his hometown. He had been there and had left. Where he was at the particular time, no one could tell.

Erebor told us that the three people who went to Ada said that they located Ojerinde's house after much difficulty. Ojerinde's people immediately concluded that the visitors from Lagos were CID men who had come to take away their townsman to Lagos. They were sure that nothing but trouble could await him in that infamous city. The people who went to Ada had come back convinced that Ojerinde was, in fact, hiding in a farmstead, one of the several which were located around Ada.

But startling news came three days after this. Ojerinde had been seen by someone in the most unlikely place anyone would have expected to find him—Lagos. Yes, Ojerinde was back in Lagos! Too good to be true. But it was true. And what was more, he was willing to meet me.

He did, again at my home one evening a few days later. I was at table with Bola and our three kids. He came in the company of Erebor and Gregory. I had them comfortably seated on the verandah where they drank beer.

"Oga, this is Mr. Ojerinde," Gregory introduced him when I came out to join them on the verandah. As usual, I left the slow-eater Bola behind in the dining room.

"Glad to meet you, my friend," I said, offering him my hand.

"I am glad to know you, sir," he said. He had a bad scar on his left cheek, most probably the aftereffect of a motor accident.

"I hear you have been away from Lagos, Mr. Ojerinde?"

"Yes, sir. I went to see my people at home."

"I hope they are well."

"Yes, sir."

"Your glass is empty," I said, inviting him to fill his glass. I realized that Bola did not approve of my offering drinks to every caller. I knew she would not like my asking the visitors to refill their glasses. But then even she ought to see the importance of filling Ojerinde with beer.

"Thank you, sir," Ojerinde said, recharging his glass.

"That fight in your house must have been very fierce," I prompted him to talk.

"It was very bad, sir."

"I understand you were in that evening."

"I was in, sir. It was truly fierce."

"You have heard, of course, what has happened to Jonathan Egbor. And to his son Paul."

"Yes, sir. I have heard."

Bola came out to the verandah. The two visitors rose to greet her, Gregory insisting on formally introducing his companion. Bola discreetly went back to the house to leave the men to continue what she knew was going to be a delicate conversation in an atmosphere uninhibited by the presence of a woman.

"Jonathan and his son are now suffering in a police cell. Very bad," I said.

"I hear so. It is very bad," Ojerinde agreed.

Then suddenly all my courage to continue the conversation evaporated. A sixth sense told me that if I continued the way we were going, the man before me would say "no" to our request that he should come out to help Jonathan. Mercifully, at that instant, Bola called me from the bedroom upstairs. I bade my visitors charge their glasses again while I went up.

"How is it going?" she asked.

"Badly."

"Badly? Why?"

"I don't know. I don't know how to continue. I think the man will say no. I suspect he will."

"Daddy, I've told you to leave this matter to Jonathan's people."

"But they have themselves brought him," I protested at the insinuation of lack of wisdom on my part.

"Listen, Daddy. Tell his companion to go and sort it out with him."

"You tell them yourself."

"What's the name of the one that lives near Jonathan?"

"Gregory," I told her, still smarting under the charge of incompetence. I left her, but she followed me out. Before I could say anything on rejoining the visitors on the verandah, Bola called out: "Mr. Gregory."

"Yes, madam."

"Jonathan sent you a message. I forgot to tell you. I'm sorry."

"Thank you, madam."

While they were away, I asked Ojerinde about his family. His wife was dead. His two sons were in secondary school, one in Ibadan, the other one at Ikirun near his hometown. Two daughters were going to primary school at Ada. They were with his wife's people.

It was at this point that Gregory came back. Not to sit, which surprised me, but to call Ojerinde away for a chat, leaving me with Erebor. Bola had gone back to the house. These women! When Gregory and Ojerinde came back, Gregory thanked me and my wife for our hospitality. He said that he and Ojerinde had agreed to discuss further "that important matter" and that they would report to me later.

Two days later I went to Mainland Police Station No. 2. I wanted to see my friend ASP Dada. I wanted him to help contact his colleagues at the Central CID to request them to expedite the police investigation. It was now more than a month since the trouble at Fasanya Street when Jonathan and his son Paul had been deprived of their liberty. I was satisfied I was not asking for anything irregular. All I wanted was someone to hurry up the processes of police investigation. They should set free the innocent men they were holding, or take them to court.

Surprise and disappointment awaited me at the police station. ASP Dada had been transferred to the Motor Traffic Division at Ilare. When last I saw him, which was only two and a half weeks before, he did not indicate that he was being transferred. Fortunately, Ilare was still in Lagos and I decided to go there at once.

I was lucky first time. He was "on seat."

"You say you want OC, sir?" a junior officer asked me. He was smart and handsome. He asked for my name and told me to wait a moment while he went in to tell the big boss inside.

While I waited in this anteroom, I looked outside at the activities of the various people milling around. Mostly the professional driver type coming to reclaim licenses that had been seized from them for traffic offences. In a number of cases, their vehicles had been seized as well and these, too, they were trying to recover. There were quite a number of other people who were not professional drivers. They also had cause to be guests of this hardly popular arm of the police.

"Come right in, sir," Dada himself came out to usher me in.

"Do you people get transferred without warning?" I asked, following him to his room.

"Oga, it was quite sudden."

"I wonder you did not tell me when last I was with you at Mainland No. 2."

"Oga, I did not know at that time."

"People should surely be given some advance warning of new postings. Time to settle a number of personal things. Schools for children and so on," I said.

"Not in the police force. Luckily this time it is still in the same town. Also it's on promotion," he announced.

"Oh, congratulations," I said enthusiastically.

"Thank you, sir."

"Good for the old school. In fact, I ought to have noticed the new uniform."

"Thank you, sir."

Eventually we got down to Jonathan and my desire that he intervene with his colleagues in the CID to expedite matters. He said the people in that department were difficult and for disciplinary reasons those in other units of the police usually kept away from them. When the authorities saw non-CID men going to the place, there was always the suspicion that the individual was up to mischief. Particularly if he belonged to the Motor Traffic Unit.

"All the same I'll see what I can do," he promised.

I thanked him.

"But you remember that man you told me would not come forward to give evidence?" he asked.

"Which of them?"

"What's his name now?" he said, sorting out the papers on his desk. He brought out a card and said: "Oh, here's his card. Martin Abiola."

"M.A. Natural. What about him?" I asked, looking at the card.

"He left here only a few minutes before you. The trouble we are in. The thing will never end."

I waited for him to tell me the sort of trouble he had with M.A. Natural.

"Apparently, one of the boys caught him with the wrong car on the road."

"You mean the wrong registration number?"

"Yes. Ah yes. LAB 6548. Of course that number should not be on the road on a Wednesday. So the boy stopped him. Don't know why they didn't sort it out the usual way," Dada said, shrugging his shoulders. The usual way was to give the police bloke a "dash."

"I know why. M.A. Natural most probably put the back of the traffic man up with his big grammar," I said, laughing.

"Exactly."

"Trust M.A. Natural to do that."

Apparently he was obliged to drive the car here. Unfortunately I wasn't in. Even after a car has been brought here under the edict, I still have the discretion to allow the person concerned to take his car away after cautioning him."

"I see."

"We just have to do that. See how many cars are dumped all over the place. We have no room to keep all of them. Part of the problem of the police. The people at the top—they sit in their air-conditioned offices and make edicts banning parking in nearly all the streets of Lagos. Yet they don't make adequate provision for where the people could park."

"I see your problem."

"Now they shift the problem onto the police. We are asked to tow away the cars. But where can we put them? Where?"

"So how do you cope with the problem?"

"You can see for yourself outside. Cars dumped all over the place. And without security, too."

"That must be bad, very bad. But what really happened to M.A. Natural eventually?"

"Him? They brought him here. I was not in. The boys insisted he just had to go and pay the edict, N100."

"Poor M.A. Natural," I said, secretly pleased by his misfortune.

"Poor M.A. Natural. Unfortunately it was a Saturday when our pay office was closed. So he couldn't pay and collect his car on Saturday."

"And has he paid now?"

"He has, today. When he brought the receipt here and the sergeant gave him the paper and the key to go and collect his car, you know what happened?"

"What happened?" I asked eagerly.

"Trouble. Real trouble," ASP Dada said, laughing. "The headlamps, the rear lamps and the external rear mirror. They had all been removed. Clean removed."

"No!"

"All gone."

"No! Not right under the nose of the police," I said in disbelief. "Who did it?"

"How would I know?"

"And what will you do about it?"

"What we will do? We shall investigate."

After some time I asked: "What will M.A. Natural do about it?"

"He threatened to sue the police. If he sues the police, we'll meet him in court. We'll investigate the theft and tell the court our findings. What else can we do? They dump all these cars here. No security whatsoever. Oga, you see any fence round us? Look," he said, leading me out to see the sea of cars awaiting collection by their owners. "Anyone can come from outside and tamper with the cars at night. Even during the daytime too. Let your man sue. We'll tell the court our own findings."

On my way home, I pondered the scandalous case of the theft that had been committed on M.A. Natural's car right under the nose of the police. Of course, it was the responsibility of the police to restore the car to the state it was in when M.A. was forced to drive it into Ilare Police Station and hand the key to the police. I was surprised at the seemingly callous attitude which my friend Dada appeared to take of the matter. However, I understood his problem.

I laughed aloud to myself at what I knew awaited M.A. Natural if he insisted on taking the matter to court. He would, of course, win the case unless his lawyer did one of the silly things that these lawyers sometimes do, which would turn a good case to a bad one.

But whatever compensation and damages he would eventually receive would be insignificant compared with the time he would have lost going to court day after day, month after month. Case adjourned today. Reason: the other side has asked for the adjournment. Case adjourned tomorrow. Reason: no counsel has appeared on either side. Case adjourned day after tomorrow. Reason: Magistrate is ill. In three years' or four years' time, my friend M.A. Natural might still be attending court.

Would it not have been better that he refitted his car, now rendered eyeless by person or persons unknown, with new lamps at his own expense and thank God for little mercies? It is said that the death which aims at cutting one's head but succeeds only in removing one's hat leaves room for gratitude to God. The fact is that whoever stripped Natural's car of its lamps could have taken away the whole car.

And if and when Martin Abiola, alias M.A. Natural, won the case against the police, the police would hardly suffer anything. It is the few million taxpayers, of whom M.A. Natural himself is one—who would suffer for it, not the police.

NINE

Meanwhile, Jonathan Egbor had been interdicted on half-pay. His full salary as a senior driver in the Housing Authority was already known to be inadequate to maintain him and his large family. And now the family were to live on half that salary. But in it all, we must thank God for little mercies. Why? Supposing the regulations were such as insisted on "no pay for no work," Jonathan, who in truth was doing no work at the time, would in fact be entitled to no pay at all. Presumably, one must thank the authors of the Public Service Code for their foresight in including provisions like this in the regulations governing the service.

Whereas Jonathan's disability was limited to interdiction on half-pay, his son Paul lost completely his temporary job as a technical assistant with a building firm. We had been able to place him with that firm only four months before the disaster that struck the family at Fasanya Street. All indications were that he was going to settle down to become a fine draughtsman before that disaster.

Our intelligence service in the police informed us when the investigation was completed. We were told that the police were preferring a charge of manslaughter against Jonathan and Paul. The case file had been sent to the State Director of Public Prosecutions for scrutiny and for the proper drafting of the charges in legal language. We awaited impatiently the return of the file to the police when the case could start in court.

But while we waited, we were not idle. We worked day and night. We worked on the citizens of Fasanya Street, not only those of them that lived at No. 22 but those who lived in the house diagonally opposite across the road. We implored them in the name of God and in the interest of justice to come forward and say at the police station the truth they told us in secret. But none of them was courageous enough to come forward. They all pleaded fear of police harassment.

All except Bintu Palmer, alias Sissy Bintu. She had confirmed to both Bola and me in the presence of Nwanna and Gregory that she saw everything as it happened that fateful day and, most important, that it was Gilbert Bassey who hit his mother Marian Bassey with the axe handle which eventually resulted in her death. Unfortunately, she had also made a statement at the police station that she had seen nothing of what happened during the fighting for the simple reason that she had locked herself up in her room when the affray started.

Sissy Bintu's change of attitude was a pleasant surprise to us all. And altogether I found her company most delightful. She said Jonathan was a very pleasant co-tenant and that she would cooperate with us to get him out of the trouble he and his son Paul were in. She was willing to write an entirely different statement for the police in replacement of the first one in which she had said that she saw nothing of what happened.

"But do you think the police will allow you to withdraw and replace your original statement with another one?" I asked her. We were in my office. She was pursuing the possibility of being registered with our authority for the supply of building materials.

"They just have to," she said. "They will. After all, they do it every day."

"Do people change statements made to the police quite often, then?" I asked.

"I cannot answer that question, Mr. Lawyer," she said, taking out a dainty mirror from her handbag and proceeding to admire her pretty face in the mirror. She stroked the inner corner of her left eyelash with the painted long nail on the index finger of her left hand. "All you want is that I should make a new statement to the police which will favour Mr. Egbor, is that not so?" she asked, putting the mirror back in the handbag.

I confirmed that that was all that we wanted.

"Haven't I told you that I will do it?"

"Of course you have. And..."

"Then you should be satisfied with that," she said, somewhat irritated.

"Of course I am satisfied," I said. She interested me in a way deeper than her promise to assist us get over one of our serious hurdles in the Jonathan Egbor case.

"Perhaps you don't trust me?" she asked teasingly, looking up from her bag. "Of course you know that nothing goes for nothing in matters like this?"

It is true nothing ever goes for nothing in our society. We had to pay for what we were arranging to get; we knew that. But to whom or to what was she alluding? Payment to the police, or to herself? Would she be demanding a bribe from us for herself so openly?

"Yes, I know we have to pay for everything, Sissy Bintu. And we are ready," I said.

"As long as you know this, brother, that nothing goes for nothing in this country, half the problem is over. And now about my registration. I want Category D," she told me.

Belo was quite happy when I told him that Sissy Bintu had consented to make a new statement to the police.

"Very good," he said. "And it means that she will also come forward to give evidence in court. Very good indeed."

"Is it true the police allow people to change statements once they have made them?" I asked.

"I know they do. And why shouldn't they?"

"But that's wrong, surely."

"Depends."

"Depends on what?" I asked.

"The way you look at it."

"Whichever way you look at it, a man making two different statements about the same incident cannot be reliable."

"A person who makes a false statement out of fright in the first instance and later decides to make a second statement after a reconsideration of the situation is a man of courage. Wouldn't you agree?"

Something told me I was being silly. When did I become the custodian of the morals of the society to argue for or against the right of a citizen to change her mind as to what she should have put on record at the police station in respect of what she saw or did not see during a fight she had witnessed? In this particular case, when we stood to gain by the proposed change of the statement with the police, it was obvious that my moralist attitude was untenable.

A few days later I again raised with my friend Belo the question of deciding on a lawyer for Jonathan and Paul. Every time I had mentioned the subject before, he had said that the exercise was premature and that we should wait till the two men were charged so that we would know the exact nature of the charge.

"Presumably there is nothing wrong in deciding on a defence lawyer now. But I warn you that you cannot brief him yet as you don't know what your man and his son are being charged with," he said.

"They are being charged with manslaughter," I told him.

"O.K. Manslaughter. Who do you have in mind?" he asked me.

"Who do I know? I'm not in the learned profession. You are."

"For manslaughter, let's see now," he said, looking through the window. We were holding the conversation in his office. "Detomi Williams?"

"Detomi Williams!" I exclaimed. "Is the case so serious that we'd be needing Detomi Williams?"

Belo laughed loud and long.

"And isn't he a SAN?" That stands for Senior Advocate of Nigeria.

"Yes. So?"

"Then he cannot appear in court without a junior, can he?"

"And you pay the fees of both himself and his junior. And I assure you his fees are as heavy as he is heavy in person. But if Nigerians believe in creating senior advocates, then they must be ready to pay them fees commensurate with their exalted position."

"Why do you think that it is on Jonathan and Paul that this exalted class of lawyers must subsist?" I asked him. Again he laughed loud and long.

"Of course I was pulling your leg," he confessed.

"But seriously, if you think we need him, I think we should engage him," I said.

"No, man. You don't want to crack a nut and order a sledge-hammer. Now let's see. There is Jonah. You know him?"

"Jonah? I don't think I do."

"And there is Idowu Peters. You know him?"

"I have heard of him."

"And there is Dapo. Dapo Oladapo Davies."

"Oh yes, I know him. Everyone does."

"He is quite an up-and-coming young man."

"Always in the papers."

"I think he's your man. I'll arrange an appointment for you with him. You know his chambers?"

"I think I do. At Denton Street, somewhere."

"Near Phoenix House."

The Esala Progressive Union had before this decided to appoint an Esala lawyer to defend Jonathan and Paul. They saw in the case soon to come to court a great booster to the importance of their hometown and their union. While Lagos and Abeokuta and Ijebu-Ode could boast of many sons of the soil who were lawyers, they too could boast of no less than seven. Five of them were practising in Bendel, their home state, while two were practising in Lagos. They had concluded that it would be invidious to pay heavy legal fees to a non-Esala man for a job that an Esala man could do for only a token fee or even free.

While I understood the tribal sentiments of Jonathan's people, I was sceptical about the ability or willingness of their man to deliver the goods. I have known in the course of many years in these matters that business is business, to be separated from tribal and kindred relations. It is when your relation knows that he is not going to charge you fees, or that you will not pay if he charges you fees for a job he is doing for you, that he goes about your job indifferently. This was why I insisted on making my own arrangement through Belo.

My uncle Papa Ota called to see me not long after this. I found him snoring heavily in one of the four armchairs on my verandah when I came back from work that afternoon. His tobacco pipe was on the drink stool and his walking-stick on the floor beside him. I decided not to disturb him and so tiptoed past him to the sitting-room.

In there, surprise number two confronted me: Raliatu. It was she and not Bola who emerged from the kitchen. She knelt down to greet me after she had placed the dish of rice on the table. Presently Bola, too, followed from the kitchen bringing the rest of the food.

"You have seen Papa Ota?" she asked.

"I have, on the verandah."

"He has been here for a long time."

"I see. Has he had something to eat?" I asked as I settled down to my meal.

"Of course he has," Bola answered belligerently. "You think Papa Ota would come to our house and I would refuse to give him food?"

I did not answer back. To do that would be to stage a scene in the presence of Raliatu and Papa Ota. The unfortunate truth was that Bola had for a long time been fighting a losing battle against relatives who came in unannounced and hoped to be fed. I had told her that there was a simple answer—ignore them. When you failed to feed them today, they would not come tomorrow.

"What kind of wife would your people think I am then?" Bola had said to my argument. "A perfectly good, reasonable wife," I had told her. "I have not married you to alienate you from the love of your relatives. How would I face the gossip that would go round that you are married to a bad woman? All I ask for is that you note all this additional feeding that I have to cope with from time to time. If you do, you will not argue so much when I occasionally ask for additional housekeeping money."

When Papa Ota awoke, I told him, briefly, what the position was about Jonathan. Not much had happened, except that we expected the case file to come back any time then from the Director of Public Prosecutions to the Commissioner of Police. After that, the police would bring the case to court.

"But have you seen the police, my son? This is why I have come from Ota to see you—that you must remember to see the police," Papa Ota said, lowering himself into the chair opposite mine. We were now in my sitting-room.

"Papa Ota, the case is not now with the police," I explained patiently. "It is now with the lawyers of government in the office of DPP. It is the lawyers of government who will now instruct the police to take the case to court."

"But my son, the police people are bad. That is what I want you to know—that the police people are bad," Papa Ota lectured me on what

116

even a child believed of the national police. "This is the reason why I have come from Ota, to let you know that you must see the police people. You must see the police in this case that they may release Jonathan and Paul."

"But Papa Ota, I have just told you that the matter is not now in the hands of the police," I said, beginning to become impatient with the old man. "I have just explained to you that the matter is now with the lawyers of government. And, and—"

"But Raliatu has come to tell me something, Kola. It is the thing that Raliatu has come to tell me that I have come to tell you, Kola. However important you are in government work, you are still my son. And I must not be afraid to talk to you," the old man said, chewing at the stem of his tobacco pipe.

"What is it that Raliatu has told you, Papa Ota?" I asked, apprehensively. The two women had discreetly retired to the kitchen.

"You want to know the thing that Raliatu has told me? I will tell you the thing that Raliatu has told me that has made me come to see you from Ota. Raliatu has come to me at Ota. She has told me that someone has told her that if we do not see the police, then the police will send her husband and her son to prison. This is the thing that Raliatu has told me. And this is the reason why I have come from Ota to tell you that we must see the police that they may not send Jonathan and Paul to prison."

I called for Raliatu from the kitchen. "Tell me, now, who is this who has told you that we must see the police? And who in the national police force is it that this person told you we must see? Is it the Inspector-General?" I asked, unable to conceal my anger.

The distraught woman broke into tears and went down on her knees. "My husband and my son, my husband and my son," she sobbed.

"Look Raliatu, we know the trouble about your husband and your son," I said, trying not to lose my patience with her. "We know the trouble. But you have now gone to Papa Ota to tell him that someone has told you that we must see someone in the police. Not so?"

"My husband, my husband," the woman continued to sob.

"Who is the person in the national police who we must see that he may not send your husband and your son to prison? I want you to tell us that," I said, getting up in anger.

"Daddy, you must understand the state of mind of Raliatu, and—"

"Now listen to me, woman," I interrupted Bola. She had joined us from the kitchen when she noticed that my voice was rising with anger. "If this woman knows someone who will get her

118

husband and her son out of trouble, she is perfectly free to take the case to her new-found adviser. And I will wash my hands of the whole thing."

"Daddy, Daddy, you must not talk like this. You know the state of mind of Raliatu," Bola pleaded with me.

Raliatu now sobbed uncontrollably on the floor. "My husband, my son," she muttered again and again.

"My son, you must listen to the words of my mouth," my uncle Papa Ota said, rising painfully from his chair. He hobbled round the woman on the floor. "You must listen to what I have to say to you, my son. You must not listen to the words of this foolish woman on the floor," he pointed to her with his walking-stick.

"What you are doing is for Jonathan. Jonathan is the son of the daughter of the sister of your father. This is the thing that I want you to remember," my uncle said as he continued to hobble round the unfortunate Raliatu who was still wailing on the floor.

"What I want to tell you is this, my son. And you must listen to the thing that I want to tell you. You must not allow the police to send the son of the daughter of the sister of your father to prison. You must understand that. You must not allow the police to send to prison the son of the daughter of the sister of your father. That would bring an everlasting stain on the name of our family. That would make us a family of shame. We do not want to become a family of shame, my son."

"My husband, my son," Raliatu sobbed on the floor.

"And I want to tell you one thing, my son," my uncle continued, still hobbling round the unhappy woman. "I want to ask you two things. Do we have a relation in an orchard and be condemned to the sucking of unripe fruit? Do we have a relation in a panel of judges and yet entertain fear that the judgment would go against us? You cannot be in the position that you are in government work and open your eyes and see the son of the daughter of the sister of your father go to prison. These are the words of my mouth."

TEN

The son of the daughter of the sister of my father.

That was the definition of the relationship between me and Jonathan Egbor according to my uncle Papa Ota. I did not know that niece of my father's who was the mother of Jonathan. I had, however, heard that there was such a niece and that she was very much older than I. I understand that a Benin road overseer who worked in the PWD in my hometown Shagamu caught the fancy of the adolescent girl in my grandfather's household. The man rode a motorcycle, which made him superior to the local lads, many of whom rode only bicycles or nothing at all. My relative apparently failed to heed the warning that she should look for a future husband among her own ethnic group in Remo, because harm invariably came to girls who married outside their own group. She ran away with the Benin man with the motorcycle. That was some four decades before.

Then Jonathan Egbor came to Ibadan some sixteen years after. My uncle Papa Ota brought him to me and told me that he was the offspring of my runaway relative. He reported to me in pretty bad English the story which he had told

Papa Ota before he decided to bring him to me. It was a story of childhood misery and unhappiness. Apparently his mother, our relation, had died giving birth to him. His road-overseer father had left the baby of bad omen with his own mother in Benin while he went with his second wife, a Benin woman, on transfer to Kano. He, too, died in Kano two years after.

The little orphan grew up in a woman's environment, doing errands and chores for his grandmother and other relations. His grandmother made him start primary school, but his attendance was intermittent as she withdrew him to follow her to nearby village markets quite often. The net result was that he had little primary education. When she died, an uncle took him away to Sapele where he worked. This uncle made him start school again, but the little boy made little progress. Besides, the uncle's wife ill-treated him. He ran away and lived as a houseboy to a succession of masters. Some treated him well; others treated him badly. He told us of a particular case where he lived for fifteen months with a young doctor in the hospital in Asaba. All went well till the doctor took a wife. As usual in these cases, the new mistress of the house took a dislike to the boy who had satisfied for fifteen months the establishment of a bachelor. Again Jonathan ran away.

He trekked westwards till he reached the big town of Ibadan—or "little Lagos" as it was called by people like him. Here he did a number of casual jobs: truck-pusher, lorry boy, and that sort of thing. Then he landed a labourer's job in the PWD. He had been doing this for only six weeks when he and the entire gang on the road construction were sacked. They were told what quite obviously was incomprehensible to them, namely, that the vote from which the job was funded had run out.

I thought that he was much too young and frail to be a labourer on the road. My uncle agreed with me. Bola and I therefore decided to take him on as a houseboy. I had a misgiving that he might behave badly to Bola in view of the blood relationship between him and me. But the boy settled down perfectly well and proved my fears wrong. After he had lived with us for three and a half years, I got him a labourer's job in the mechanical workshops of the PWD in Ibadan. There he soon learnt the mechanic's trade and driving. And when I was transferred to Lagos, I got him a job as a driver-mechanic in the Housing Authority.

ELEVEN

We heard that the police had concluded their investigations and had sent their findings and recommendations to the office of the Director of Public Prosecutions—DPP for short. The big boss with the awe-inspiring title. He it was who had to decide whether or not Jonathan Egbor and his son Paul should be set free or taken to court. And if they were to be taken to court, he had to decide whether they were to be charged with manslaughter or with murder.

The police had concluded their investigation without replacing the original statement of Bintu Palmer with another one that would be more favourable to our case. I understand that our contact in the police came out with a more acceptable proposition: that the police would discard Mrs. Palmer's original statement and not ask for a replacement, as they had decided not to use her as a witness. This was a more straightforward proposition, as the celebrity of 22 Fasanya Street was now all ours. I kept in touch with her. It was important that I should. And besides, it was pleasant doing so.

The Director of Public Prosecutions took ages studying the file of Jonathan and Paul. I had expected that in a week or two, or in a month, we would have a decision sent down to the police from the office of the DPP. But no. Day after day, week after week, we waited. And month after month, we waited. We were told why we were waiting: the DPP was still studying the case file of Jonathan and Paul. And while the big boss allegedly studied the case file, citizens Jonathan and Paul Egbor remained in police custody.

Just who did the police think they were kidding? Who did not know that the DPP, the big chief, was much too big to be personally involved in the case of a mere driver and his son? You might think that because they had been in police custody for several weeks, that ought to be sufficient reason for the big boss to intervene personally and expedite the administrative processes that would enable the case to come to court and the Magistrate to release Jonathan and Paul to us on bail. But no. If anyone believes that the DPP, himself, should personally look into the case of every Jonathan and Paul deprived of their freedom of movement for a few months, then that person needs to do some rethinking.

Our secret intelligence continued to be busy in the DPP's office. Through him came information about the movement and non-movement of the important file. Yes, it occasionally moved, as files sometimes do on the desks of public servants. But most times it did not move, as when files so often get conveniently placed in the pending tray, labouring under the over-burden of new files that grow in number on top of them with each day. Then occasionally the file surfaced again and, sometimes, moved again.

How I wished that I knew someone who knew someone who knew the big boss, to bring to his august notice how much the sparing of a mere twenty minutes of his precious time to look into the case of these lowly citizens might easily cut some twenty days, possibly twenty weeks, from the length of time that these two citizens, father and son, would remain deprived of their freedom! But of course not. No one must ever think of doing a thing like that. For to do that would be interpreted as interfering with the course of justice. That was why we were resigned to our fate, waiting day after day, week after week, and month after month, for a decision to come down from the office of the DPP while we helplessly watched Jonathan and Paul suffer in police custody.

"You must continue to be a man," I enjoined Jonathan one day at the premises of the Mainland Magistrates Court. He and several other men being held in police custody had been brought to the Magistrates Court in the "Black Maria." The police had come to seek the magistrate's approval for remanding the men in custody for another period of one month while the police investigation continued or, as in the case of Jonathan and Paul, while the Director of Public Prosecutions' decision concerning the charge was awaited.

"But master, we suffer too much in custody," Jonathan said mournfully. "Master, when I did not kill anyone, why should police people punish me so much?"

"Take heart, Jonathan. That is all I can say now," I confessed helplessly.

We were all in a group surrounding the Black Maria. The police allowed me, Raliatu, and Gregory to talk to Jonathan and Paul. They also allowed a few other favoured persons to see the other men in custody. They threatened to beat with their batons other relatives who wished to talk to the unfortunate men in their charge.

"You are alright, Paul?" I asked, trying to escape further embarrassing complaints from Jonathan.

"Yes, sir," Paul replied, nearly choking on the rice which Raliatu had brought. The police had turned a blind eye to this.

Then Mrs. Bintu Palmer came to us. I was surprised to see her.

"Madam, you see now they say I killed Mrs. Bassey," Jonathan answered her greeting with the agony on his mind. "Madam, don't you remember how that boy Gilbert hit his own mother with the axe handle? Now they say I and Paul killed the woman."

"That's alright, Jonathan," I said, as his voice was rising.

128

"Everybody knew who killed Mrs. Bassey," Bintu Palmer said. "You wait, Mr. Egbor. When we get to court and the case begins, then we shall hear the truth."

"Please, master, tell Papa Paul to eat something," Raliatu pleaded with me.

"Jonathan, why aren't you eating?" I asked him.

And without saying a word, he accepted the spoon Raliatu held out to him. He moved near to Paul and joined in the meal.

"I didn't know you were coming, Sissy Bintu?" I turned to Mrs. Palmer.

"Don't you know I have a case in court today?"

"What case?"

"Didn't I tell you what my steward did to me?" she asked. As usual, she was smartly dressed, this time in a blue, V-necked frock that exposed more than enough of her beautiful breasts. She wore a pair of goggles that made it difficult for you to tell whether she was looking at you or looking somewhere else.

"No, you didn't. What was it he did to you?"

"Packed away all my trinkets. And my money, too," she said. Her perfume pervaded the air.

"At Fasanya Street?" I asked.

"No. When I was still living with Mr. Palmer at Ikoyi."

"That must have been some time ago," I said, since I knew that Palmer went on transfer quite some time back.

"Oh, terrible. I've been in this trouble since 1974. Real trouble."

I moved away a little from the cluster of people round the Black Maria. I beckoned to her to do the same. Even though there was nothing particularly secret in what she was telling me, I thought we could all the same do with a bit of confidentiality and quiet.

"Apparently the rogue was caught," I observed, leaning against the bonnet of a car.

"Yes. He was caught by the police. He and his accomplices. And they are in court now."

"Well. That's something at least for the police. People say they never, never catch thieves. And—"

"Well, really they couldn't but catch this lot. They practically walked to the police and begged to be caught."

"Really?"

"And since 1974, when the wretches were charged, it has been a case of 'come today, come tomorrow.' I'm tired of the whole thing. I'm fed up. And now the case has been adjourned again."

"Till when, Sissy?" I asked.

"Till 25 July. I'm thoroughly fed up. But it is to be judgment that day."

"That's good. And the outlook?"

"Very good. It's quite clear that the boy stole the money and the trinkets. And that his accomplices received them."

By an interesting coincidence, the date to which Sissy Bintu's case was adjourned was the date on which Jonathan and Paul were brought to the Magistrate for a renewal of the remand warrant to keep them in police custody. I had been with Jonathan and Paul for a few minutes among the usual crowd around the Black Maria. I then hurried back to the courtroom. I was keen on hearing the Magistrate read the judgment.

The Magistrate was still busy in his chambers when I got back. Most probably signing the document that would keep poor Jonathan and Paul in custody for yet another month. The lawyers chatted and laughed. How casual these men of the "learned profession" appeared in the way they discussed cases and other matters which appeared to me important and grave.

"You have a case here, Mr. Banjo?" a lawyer acquaintance asked me.

"No. I'm interested in Mrs. Palmer's case."

"Oh, I see," the lawyer said mischievously, looking in the direction of the gorgeous Sissy Bintu.

"You think Sissy Bintu has a good case?" I asked him.

"Of course she has. Even though we have to make allowance for the vagaries of the law. I think on balance the police have a good case."

The police had a good case! That reminded me that, in fact, it was not a case between Mrs. Palmer and her steward and associates, but between the Commissioner of Police and those culprits. It was an irony of the imported legal system that Mrs. Bintu Palmer, the woman who was most concerned in the case, was only in fact a police witness instead of being made the principal character.

"Presumably there are vagaries in the law, then?" I asked him.

"I'm afraid there are. Not as exact a science as your engineering, where you measure everything with your slide rule," he said, laughing. "And much depends on what the Magistrate believes and what he does not believe."

"I see."

"And also the way the prosecution put their case. I'm afraid the police are usually inefficient in the prosecution of criminal cases in the magistrate courts. The Bar Association has recommended that only men of the legal profession should prosecute cases in these courts. But government thinks we only want to make money for members of the Bar."

"I see, I see," I commented.

"Most magistrates don't think the police are reliable. They would rather resolve a doubt in favour of an accused person."

We were interrupted by three knocks on the door leading to the Magistrate's chambers. The knocking was loud, as if it had been produced by something like the handle of a machete or the butt of a gun applied with some force to the door. We both looked in the direction of the door.

"Court!" a gruff voice shouted from behind the door.

The babbling in the court ceased. Everyone rose as the Magistrate came in through the door. He took a few short but dignified steps to his chair, turned round and faced the main court. He then bowed gravely and took his seat. This was a signal for the lawyers and for the spectators to sit quietly in their seats.

For the first half-hour or so, the Magistrate dealt with what in legal circles they called "overnight cases." Mostly traffic offences and fighting in public places. In each case, the accused person was allowed bail and a date was fixed for a hearing that was mutually convenient to the Magistrate, the defence counsel, and the police prosecutor.

The first part of the Magistrate's judgment in the case of Commissioner of Police versus Stephen Okon and two others was a long review of the case interlarded with legal terms and legal precedents quoted mostly by the defence counsel. The Magistrate read it all, appearing to care little as to whether or not people in the court followed what he was saying. He stumbled in his reading from time to time, evidence of difficulty in reading his own writing. I wondered why judgments are not typed, which would make reading easier. That, of course, would make it possible for the typist to leak the judgment to the litigants! And he would, in Nigeria!

"I now turn to Exhibits J, K, L, M, and N," the Magistrate was reading. "These are one gold necklace, one gold pendant, one pair of gold earrings, one gold brooch, and one lady's wristwatch. All these were identified by the third prosecution witness, Bintu Palmer, as belonging to her. I do not believe the evidence of the second accused that these pieces of jewellery found in his house belonged to his sister. Nor do I believe the evidence of the fourth defence witness, Anna Okafor, who said the exhibits belonged to her. I believe that both the second defendant and the fourth defence witness conspired to tell lies to mislead the court. I therefore order that exhibits

J, K, L, M, and N be released to the third prosecution witness, Bintu Palmer."

I saw Mrs. Palmer's beautiful bosom rise under the beige lace blouse as she heaved a long sigh of relief and happiness at this pronouncement. I whispered congratulations to her.

"I now come to Exhibit R. This is the Barclays Bank Savings Account Book No. BBN 7651. This account was opened by the third accused, Charles Akpan, on 23 February 1974, with a sum of ₦ 180. I have given consideration to the evidence of the third accused that this sum represented the accumulation of savings from his salary over many months, which he originally deposited with his sister. I have also given consideration to the argument of the prosecution that from a salary of ₦ 70.00 a month it was not possible for the third accused person to save a sum of ₦ 180 which he deposited in his savings account on 23 February 1974. I am particularly impressed by the point made by the prosecution that it was the day following the larceny and the disappearance of Exhibits K, L, M, N, and R from the house of the third prosecution witness at 25A Adeyemi Lawson Road at Ikoyi that the third accused opened this account.

"Yet the prosecution has failed to show the link between the ₦180 allegedly in ₦ 10 notes missing at 25A Adeyemi Lawson Road at Ikoyi and the ₦ 180 that was deposited in the bank account of the third accused, Charles Akpan. The prosecution has failed to show that the ₦ 180 deposited in the bank account were in ₦ 10 notes and that these notes were the actual notes removed from 25A Adeyemi Lawson Road."

Mrs. Palmer groaned aloud. I cautioned her in a whisper to control her emotions, lest she be held for contempt of court.

"In these circumstances, therefore, I hold that the prosecution has failed to prove beyond all reasonable doubt that the money found in the bank account of the third accused person was the same money allegedly stolen from the third prosecution witness. I therefore order that Exhibit R be returned to the third accused, Charles Akpan."

Mrs. Palmer groaned. I was apprehensive.

"I find the first accused, Stephen Okon, guilty on the first, second, and fourth counts. I find the second accused, Johnson Obi, guilty on the first and second counts. I find the third accused, Charles Akpan, not guilty of any of the two counts of the charges preferred against him. He is therefore discharged and acquitted."

Bintu Palmer rose to go out without waiting for the Magistrate to finish pronouncing sentence on the first two accused persons. Her sobs, in spite of her effort to muffle them, were audible even to the Magistrate. I followed her out of a sense of gallantry. In the court corridor, she broke down in tears.

"Take it easy," I consoled her, trying to steer her further along the corridor away from where her sobbing could still be heard in the court, a thing that I thought could make the Magistrate order her to be arrested.

"See my trouble. See my trouble, after all this time," she sobbed. "See my shame. Yet the money was actually found in the boy's bank account..."

"Control yourself, Mrs. Palmer. If even..."

At this point, there was a tremendous yell in the courtroom. Apparently, the Magistrate had pronounced sentence on the two convicted persons and had risen. A moment after, the door burst open and the crowd of Charles Akpan supporters trooped out, shouting in ecstasy. I quickly dragged Bintu Palmer out of their way. But they saw her.

"Look at her, Asewo," one of them said in derision.

"You see your shame now. You think you are the only one that can get money?" another said.

"It is your mother at home you are talking about," Bintu Palmer answered back, to my embarrassment.

"Mrs. Palmer, please," I pleaded with her, trying to lead her away from the crowd. "You mustn't come down to their level."

"See my shame. See how that Magistrate has shamed me," she sobbed again.

"Prostitute. Go to the Oyinbo sailors. You get more money than ₦ 180 tonight," one of the ruffians said, to the amusement of all. She was now surrounded by her own supporters. They all tried to quieten her.

"You have transport, Mrs. Palmer?" I asked.

"Yes, I have. Oh, how I've suffered. Oh God. It is not these, these, these bastards. It is the Magistrate that has so shamed me today. And I will, I will, I will show him that I am a Lagos-born woman."

"Sissy Bintu, please," I cautioned her against such bad language.

"That Ara-oke they made Magistrate. I don't know why they made the useless man a Magistrate in this Lagos. Say I am a bastard if I don't get him sacked in this Lagos."

TWELVE

Twenty days after the case in which Bintu Palmer was humiliated, the case of Commissioner of Police versus Jonathan Egbor and Paul Egbor did come to Magistrate Court No. 3 at the Mainland. That was on 14 August 1975, exactly seven months and seventeen days after the fight at 22 Fasanya Street, and seven months and sixteen days after both men had been deprived of their freedom.

All along, our secret intelligence had indicated that Jonathan and Paul would be charged with manslaughter, and not murder. We were ready—myself and Jonathan's people—to bail him and Paul. I knew they had brought some money, withdrawn from the scholarship savings account of the Esala Progressive Union two days before. I had originally thought it would not be necessary for them to use the money in bailing Jonathan, for I thought the court would accept me as surety for both of them. But later I was told that as a public servant, I was not allowed to stand bail for anyone. In any case, I still brought to court the conveyance of my house at Ilare. That, I thought, might be acceptable. Surely there couldn't be anything wrong with a public servant pledging his landed property to bail someone.

That was how we prepared to bail Jonathan and Paul at court that day, and how we all looked forward to the event. I was a little late getting to the court. The Magistrate was already on seat, but he was still busy with the "overnights" when I came. I had hardly taken my seat when one of Jonathan's people, Isaiah Erebor, called me out. Out in the corridor, he gave me the stunning news.

"It is murder, sir. They are charging him with murder, sir," he said, nearly in tears.

"What d'you say?" I asked in disbelief.

"They are charging both of them with murder, sir," he repeated.

"It's manslaughter. The SP himself..." I stopped here. I could not give out details of secret information which had been given me in strict confidence.

"Even our own man in the police told us till yesterday that it would be manslaughter. But the prosecutor himself told Isaiah this morning that it is murder."

We both looked at each other. "That's terrible," I said.

"Very bad, sir. Will they allow bail for murder?"

"No, they won't," I said in disappointment.

"So I am told. What can we do now?"

"I'll ask our lawyer."

But Dapo Oladapo Davies, Esq., Bachelor of Laws, Barrister at Law of the Supreme Court of Nigeria, was not in court that day. Yet it was the day we had all awaited so eagerly. In fairness to him, however, Dapo Oladapo Davies had told me when I had called at his office to remind him about the case coming to court on 14 August that he would not be in court that day. He had said that he did not need to be in court because he was certain that the case would not be started that day. The prosecution would be certain to be asking for a long adjournment. He would, however, be sending his junior to court.

The "lawyer son of the soil" whom the Esala Progressive Union had hoped would do the case had not been available. He had returned from Europe and had gone back again. Apparently, he had found business there more lucrative than the practice of law and, like many before him, was already abandoning the practice of the learned profession for other pursuits.

To my disappointment, the junior that Dapo Oladapo Davies promised did not turn up either. I had to make a hurried arrangement with one of the lawyers in court that morning. I did not remember his name, but I knew he was a friend of my younger brother's. And since the case was not going on that day, he couldn't do much harm.

"You, Jonathan Egbor, are charged with the unlawful killing of Marian Bassey at 22 Fasanya

Street, Surulere, in the Magisterial District of Lagos, on or about the 28th day of January 1975, thereby committing an offence under section 319 of the Criminal Code, Cap 31, of the Laws of Lagos State. Are you guilty or not guilty?" the clerk read out the charge.

Jonathan in the dock regarded him with amazement as he heard him read out the charge. He opened his mouth and then closed it. He shook his head and looked away.

"Are you guilty or not guilty?" the clerk asked again.

"Guilty? How can I be guilty? I did not kill anybody. I was only..."

"First accused pleads not guilty, Your Worship," the clerk announced over his shoulders to the Magistrate, who at that time was busy writing where he sat importantly on the bench.

"You, Paul Egbor, are charged with the unlawful killing of Marian Bassey at 22 Fasanya Street, Surulere, in the Magisterial District of Lagos, on or about the 28th day of January 1975, thus committing an offence punishable under section 319 of the Criminal Code, Cap 31, of the Laws of Lagos State. Are you guilty or not guilty?"

"I am not guilty," Paul said in a voice surprisingly clear in the circumstances.

"Second accused pleads not guilty, Your Worship," the clerk announced disinterestedly to the magistrate. His Worship wrote on without looking up from what he was writing. From him, I looked at Raliatu. She was busy reciting to herself some incantations where she sat. After some time, the magistrate looked up.

"Your Worship, I appear for the prosecution," the state counsel announced, mentioning his name as Pedro. "I shall, however, be asking Your Worship for an adjournment. I still have to study the case. I knew about it only this morning."

"You are always wanting adjournments," the magistrate said, looking at the State Counsel. "You are never ready for your cases, Mr. Pedro."

"Not my fault, Your Worship. If one man is doing the work of four, Your Worship..."

"And getting the salary of four, I presume?" His Worship asked, laughing.

They all laughed all the lawyers in the court.

"No, that's the point, Your Worship. One man doing the work of four, but getting the salary of one," the State Counsel said, looking round the rank of lawyers. Again they all laughed. It no doubt was funny. But God knew I did not consider the situation funny at all. Jonathan and Paul were going to remain in custody for a long, long time more. And all that these people these learned people could do was to laugh.

"Your Worship, I hold the brief for Mr. Dapo Oladapo Davies," our relief lawyer announced, also mentioning his name. "We too will be asking for a long adjournment, like my learned friend, to enable us to take instruction from our clients."

The case was fixed for 25 September. Another six weeks in custody for Jonathan and Paul. Good God!

A greater complication in Jonathan being charged with murder instead of manslaughter was that he was now transferred, together with Paul, from the police cell at the Central CID to the Island Prison. Here, in this place of horror, both of them were held together with men who were already convicted, and subjected to the same terribly harsh treatment to which these convicts were subjected. And what was worse, they were kept separated, in different cells.

"Master, you see my trouble now. See what they are doing to me for something I never did," Jonathan cried the first day I went to visit him at the Island Prison. Official visiting here was more difficult, as the prison authorities observed strict security regulations to prevent the escape of prisoners and accused persons in their charge, or the passing to them of implements which they could use for cutting their way out of their cell, or the making of things which they could use for committing suicide.

We talked to each other through a hatch some two metres wide and one metre high in the wall that separated the chief warder's room from what most probably was a hall used for this very purpose. The opening was made secure by strong iron bars embedded in the concrete sill at the bottom and the lintel at the top of the hatch.

"You must be brave, Jonathan," I told him.

"But master, not manslaughter they first told us they are charging us with?" he asked. "And did they not say then that you can bail us?"

"I know," I said. I had practically assured him it was going to be manslaughter. Now I felt guilty and ashamed. I felt as if I was responsible for upgrading the charge from manslaughter to murder.

He said something which I did not hear. How could one hear properly in the circumstances with six or so different conversations going on at one and the same time? For we visitors on our side of the hatch sat on one bench, each facing on the other side of the wall the inmate he or she had come to see, and each person was shouting his conversation as loudly as possible so as to drown the conversation of the other people around him. The babbling on both sides of the hatch was reminiscent of a madhouse.

"What did you say, Jonathan?" I asked him.

"I say that you should help me more, master," he shouted.

"We are doing our best, Jonathan."

"Tell the lawyer to beg the Magistrate to hear the case quickly. Master, we are suffering in this place."

"I am doing my best. You just take courage, Jonathan. You just have to," I consoled him.

"But master, how can I stay here for another six weeks like this?" He broke down in heavy, manly sobs. So did his son Paul. And so did I. Yes, I too cried at the needless suffering of the innocent. I was not ashamed of my action. Did Jesus himself not weep once?

Now more than ever we had need of Emmanuel Ojerinde. He was now our man. Isaiah Erebor and Gregory Eregie came to tell me of their agreement with him three days after the meeting in my house. Apparently, Ojerinde was already having problems before Marian Bassey died. He was already in arrears with his rent and had been given notice to quit by the landlord. He was ready to give evidence for Jonathan. But we had to help him out of his trouble.

He required ₦65 to pay the landlord at 22 Fasanya Street, to liquidate the debt he had owed for five months in respect of his ₦13-a-month room. He had already found new accommodation at Abule Oja. The new landlord wanted twelve months' payment in advance for a room, at a monthly rent of ₦18. He said he had begged the new landlord, who had agreed to reduce the twelve months to six months. So he needed ₦108 for that. In all, therefore, his immediate requirement was ₦173.

Finally, he insisted that we realize that by undertaking to come to court to say what he had seen at 22 Fasanya Street on that fateful day, he was taking a tremendous risk. He would be a marked man by the relatives of the deceased woman, Marian Bassey. Should anything happen to him, what would become of his children? He wanted a signed agreement in which we would guarantee to pay the educational expenses of his four children up to and including secondary school in the event of his dying as a result of his having given evidence in the case of Commissioner of Police versus Jonathan Egbor and Paul Egbor.

And the evidence of Bintu Palmer became vital now. I arranged an appointment with her to take her to the chambers of Dapo Oladapo Davies for a rehearsal of her evidence. That was after I had checked that she had been registered as a building contractor with the Housing Authority.

THIRTEEN

Preliminary Investigation! That was the new horror hurled at the case of Commissioner of Police versus Jonathan Egbor and Paul Egbor. This new horror is called PI in legal circles. Barrister Dapo Oladapo Davies first told me of it when I was pressurizing him to go to visit Jonathan and Paul at the Island Prison to hear their case from their own mouths. He told me there was no desperate hurry about this particular aspect of the matter.

"No hurry? Why is that?" I asked him. We were in his chambers. And I thought we were all in a hurry for the blessed case to be over.

"The DPP people are not ready to start the case yet. Even..."

"But we can at least get ready our own side of the case," I said.

"That's just what we mustn't do. You see, what will be done at the Magistrates' Court is just the Preliminary Investigation. When the proceedings are finished at the Magistrates' Court, the case goes up to the High Court. There, the whole thing starts all over again."

"No!" I exclaimed.

"I'm afraid so. You will wonder why they hold the PI in the first instance," he continued. "That's what we lawyers always wonder, too. An absolute waste of time."

"You mean when this case does start and is finished in the Magistrates' Court at Yaba, the two men cannot be discharged and acquitted?" I asked in amazement.

"No. They cannot be discharged and acquitted. Neither can they be convicted. The Magistrate is not competent to do either of these in a murder case."

After some time I asked: "If that is so, why doesn't the case go to the High Court in the first instance? Why does the Magistrate have to meddle in a case in which he has no competence?"

"To be honest, I don't know. I don't think anyone else does. I doubt if the DPP or even the Chief Justice himself does. It's the usual procedure, however. Most cumbersome. And we lawyers hate it. It's a damn waste of time. We always send juniors to the Magistrates' Court to cover the proceedings at a PI. We give them instructions, strict instructions, just to listen and record. They do not put our own witnesses in the box. Nor do they cross-examine the prosecution witnesses."

"Why?" I asked, recovering slowly from the disappointment of my new discovery.

"We do not want to give away to the prosecution the strategy of our own defence. If we say anything in the lower court, the State Counsel will know our strategy, and that would not be good for our case."

"I see."

"It is at the real trial at the High Court that we spring our surprises. And I'll see to it that we'll have real surprises. Which means that we must work hard on these witnesses. I hear Mr. Martin Abiola is one of them?"

"M. A. Natural? Yes. But I'm afraid he won't play ball. I've told Belo that."

"I think he will. We lawyers know how to deal with reluctant witnesses."

"How?"

"Secret of the trade, I'm afraid. Three years in the university, and another one year at the Nigerian Law School. After you've done that, we can begin to share the secrets with you. And talking seriously, sir, we must get our man M.A. Natural. And the other two. We just have to get them. No other way, I'm afraid. Incidentally, is Mrs. Palmer still with us?"

"Yes. She is still with us. But she has been unable to convince M.A. Natural to come with her."

On my way, I pondered this new development. The Preliminary Investigation thing. If the procedure the Magistrate was about to start was the Preliminary Investigation, just what had the police at the Central CID been doing? Presumably, that was the Preliminary Preliminary Investigation (PPI). And what had the police at the Mainland Police Station No. 2 been doing? Preliminary, Preliminary, Preliminary Investigation (PPPI or P^{3}I). What a ridiculous waste of time!

You would think that the prosecution, that is, the police and the big boss, the DPP would at least get on with one Preliminary Investigation and get done with it. But no. They were all just dragging their feet, just fiddling while the innocent rotted away in custody, incarcerated with men already convicted of crimes against society and subjected to terrible living conditions.

Once again, week after week and month after month, we waited for the Preliminary Investigation to start. And week after week, and month after month, we waited in vain. Not that we did not go to court. Of course we did. Each day to which the case was adjourned we went to court, but only to be told the same nasty story: the DPP was not ready to go on with the case yet. The DPP, of course, was an important person! Besides, a murder case is a very important case. So we just had to wait till the big boss, the DPP, was ready.

On one of the occasions when we attended court only to be told the usual story that the case of Jonathan and Paul could not go on because the prosecution was not yet ready, the Magistrate was very angry with the prosecution in another case.

"You come here every day to tell the same story that you are not ready," the Magistrate rebuked the prosecutor. He was an inspector of police. "Why don't you get your cases ready before rushing to court? This poor man has been coming to court for nine months now."

"Not nine months, Your Worship," the lawyer for the unfortunate accused person corrected His Worship. "It is—er—twenty-three months that we have been coming to this court, wasting our time. Nearly two years, Your Worship." These lawyer boys they talk of their clients not in the third person singular, but in the first person plural.

"Yes, nearly two years," the Magistrate said angrily from the exalted bench. "And I understand the accused person lives in Calabar."

"This is quite so, Your Worship," again the defending counsel rode on the wave of magisterial displeasure against the prosecution. "I would respectfully urge this honourable court to discharge the accused person. Your Worship has the power under the law."

"I know I have the power. And that's precisely what I'm going to do if the prosecution is not ready with its case the next time it comes up."

It was confirmed by Belo that the Magistrate could discharge an accused person in such circumstances if he was satisfied that the accused had been suffering needlessly because of the prosecution not being ready to start its case. That would apply to minor criminal offences like driving dangerously, or driving without proper documents. The magistrate would not throw out a murder case for this reason, unfortunately.

Then Bola took the case of Jonathan and Paul to God. "Prayer, Daddy, is the only answer," she told me seriously one evening after supper. It was the end of another day when we had been to court and had been told the usual story that the case could not go on.

"Yes, Mummy," I said, looking at her inquiringly. For I knew she had included Jonathan and Paul in her supplications to God every morning and every night. While I would not commit myself on the efficacy or otherwise of prayer, I was now considering what the justification was for this additional interest in prayer.

"Miserable thou art, whosoever thou be or whithersoever thou turn unless thou turn thyself to God," she read out to me a passage from a little black book of prayers.

"Yes," I said. "We have been praying. And we'll continue to pray. But I think God is taking a rather long time answering our prayer."

"Daddy!"

I took the hint. I must not blaspheme, whatever the temptation. Besides, I must not confuse the timescale. The thirteen months in which Jonathan and Paul had been suffering, deprived of their freedom, might be long in the time units which we humans use. But a thousand years in the sight of God are only like an evening gone; a thousand, thousand years are mere seconds on the divine timescale. So, I saw the need for continued patience in waiting for God to come to the aid of Jonathan and Paul.

"Daddy, we are taking the case of Jonathan and Paul to God," again Bola enlightened me. I now understood.

The following Sunday morning we worshipped in our church, St. Nicholas.

"A woman member of this church is asking for the united prayer of this congregation for God's blessing on two people dear to her and her family, who are now kept in prison custody for a crime that they did not commit," the Vicar announced at the time for special prayers. "She is requesting the united prayer of the people of God for the judicial authorities to speed up the processes of law to enable the case to be heard quickly in court and the two dear people be set free to join their family. She is also praying that God may give courage to those who know the truth about what happened but are now afraid to come forward and speak the truth in this case. The member has enclosed a ₦5 note with her request. Let us take to God our Father this special request of our dear sister in Christ, remembering that with the Lord our God all things are possible and that without him nothing is possible. Let us remember that man's extremity is God's opportunity. A male member of the congregation will lead us in prayer. Let us pray."

"Almighty Jah Jehovah, the same yesterday, the same today, the same forever." It was the voice of one of the Elders of the church. The final call for prayer had hardly left the lips of our Vicar before this man's voice came into action, completely drowning the voice of another worshipper who too had started on his own prayer in response to the call from the vicar.

"You are the mighty One who rides on the waves with the dexterity with which a warrior rides on a horse. You are the great Deliverer who delivered Moses and your chosen ones on the distant shores of the Red Sea from the hosts of Pharaoh, the wicked King of Egypt. We call upon you at this solemn hour of prayer to deliver from the machinations of the wicked men of this world the two dear ones on behalf of whom we now kneel in prayer before your throne of grace."

"Amen," the congregation shouted in unison.

"The God of Abraham, God of Isaac and God of Jacob. You it was who piloted the Ark of Noah over the great tempest and flood. You it was who shielded him and all his household through the many, many days of that tempest. The Almighty One of Israel, do not allow our ship to founder in this world's tempestuous sea."

"Amen."

"God of our fathers, do not allow us and those dear to us to perish in this world's turbulent sea."

"Amen."

"In Sodom and Gomorrah, you remembered and did not forget your chosen ones in those cities of sin. You delivered Lot and his household from destruction. You, the great Deliverer, we pray you at this solemn hour to deliver our dear ones from the machinations and wickedness of the evil men now scheming to have them imprisoned even though they have committed no crime."

"Amen. Amen."

"You, Almighty God, the one with very long arms, able to bring out safe your chosen ones from the deepest abyss of danger; you who saved your prophet Elijah from the schemings of the wicked Queen and ancient witch Jezebel; you who saved Shadrach, Meshach and Abednego from the furnace of immeasurable heat, we pray to you at this solemn hour of prayer not to allow our dear one to be consumed in the furnace fuelled by the wicked men of this wicked world."

"Amen. Amen."

"You brought out Daniel safe from the lion's den in those days of old in the city of Nebuchadnezzar the King. Let it please you to bring out safe and speedily our dear ones from the prison place where wicked people have now kept them even though they have not committed any crime."

"Amen. Amen."

"And Father Almighty..."

"Amen, Amen."

"Lord, God of Hosts..."

"Amen, Amen..."

"You brought out Jonah alive and safe after living for three days and three nights in the stomach of a fish..."

"Amen, Amen."

"Send to our dear ones now kept unjustly in prison custody a fish that will keep them alive and safe..."

"Amen, Amen."

"You, Almighty God..."

"Amen, Amen."

"You are the Supreme Judge of the whole world. You are the Judge that is greater than all the judges of Lagos and all the Judges of Ibadan and all the Judges of the white man's country put together..."

"Amen, Amen."

"We pray you to make the judge try this case speedily, and set our dear ones free."

"Amen, Amen."

"We pray you not to allow evil men to come forward to give false evidence against your servants now suffering unjustly in prison custody."

"Amen, Amen."

"Rather Lord, God Almighty, let all who come forward to give evidence remember the Seventh Commandment given to us your children by your servant Moses on Mount Sinai that we must not bear false witness."

"Amen, Amen."

"And now God, we pray in respect of those who know the truth, those who are now afraid..."

I had up till this moment followed reasonably the prayer. I noticed that Bola, who sat next to me, followed even more devotedly, judging by her loud "amens." But at this stage, my eyes wandered to M.A. Natural where he sat in the special pew of the pastor's warden, impressive in his blue robes, which went very well with the blue suit underneath.

"...give them the courage to come forward to tell the truth they know, that the dear ones may be set free from prison custody and rejoin their family."

"Amen, Amen."

And M.A. Natural—real name Martin Abiola, pastor's warden of our church, St. Nicholas—joined in the amen chorus in response to that supplication! Were the words of the prayer striking the right chord in his mind, I wondered.

The answer to that united prayer of the people of God was immediate and sure. On the Wednesday following that Sunday, both the radio and the papers announced that the Chief Justice had visited a number of prisons both in Lagos and elsewhere in the States. He had been moved by the appalling conditions in which both convicted prisoners and accused persons still awaiting trial were kept in these prisons. He had expressed the hope that the living conditions of these unfortunate people would be improved and their sufferings alleviated.

As a result of that visit, five accused persons who had been held in custody for a total of eleven years between them at the Mainland Prisons were set free. The argument was that even if found guilty and convicted, the maximum terms of imprisonment to which these men would be sentenced would not be longer than the time they had already spent in custody at the Mainland Prison.

Unfortunately, Jonathan and Paul were not set free. But the Chief Justice directed that their case and the case of two others held in custody in the Island Prison should now go straight to the High Court, thus short-circuiting the unwanted, needless, time-wasting Preliminary Investigation. We read this decision in the press a few days after the Chief Justice arrived in Lagos from Kaduna. And we were very, very happy. Who says God does not listen to the prayers of his people?

FOURTEEN

Three weeks after the Chief Justice's directive that the case of Jonathan and Paul be transferred to the High Court, we had yet another shock. Raliatu came to us at Surulere on Sunday night after she had visited her husband at the Island Prison that morning, and he had told her that he and Paul were to appear at the Magistrates' Court as usual the following Tuesday. It was true that it was that Tuesday to which the case had been adjourned at the last hearing, which, of course, was no hearing at all. I asked Raliatu if the prison authorities were not aware of the ruling of the Chief Justice that the Magistrates' Court should wash their slow-moving hands clean of our case. That, of course, was a stupid question, as Raliatu was the last person to know what the prison authorities were aware of and what they were not. Raliatu did not know anything about anything, except reproduction and cooking.

My attempt to contact both my unpaid legal adviser Belo and our lawyer Dapo Oladapo Davies, to let them know of the latest development, failed. Both were out of Lagos. I went to court on Tuesday, certain that nothing would happen, but ready to keep a watchful eye on the goings-on. True enough, the case was called, and Jonathan and Paul were, as usual, led into the dock.

To my greatest surprise, a gentleman rose from the rank of lawyers. He announced that he was appearing for the prosecution. My God! The Director of Public Prosecutions had at last sent someone to prosecute the case. They were now trying to impress people that they were efficient only after the Chief Justice, the biggest of the big bosses, had already directed that the case be transferred to the High Court. Efficiency indeed!

"No counsel appearing for the defence?" the Magistrate asked, after he had written something in his book from which he now looked up. He looked round the rank of lawyers. "No counsel appearing for the defence?" the Magistrate again asked.

At this stage, I was worried. Was this case to go on at the Magistrates' Court after all and Dapo Oladapo Davies nowhere to be found? I was tempted for a brief moment to get up and explain to His Worship why our lawyer was not in court. But I knew at once that I must not do that lest I be charged with contempt of court, which could land me in gaol. I must keep quiet. For I had no status in the case, and I was no learned friend!

Then one learned counsel rose. "Your Worship, I speak as a friend of the court," he said. "I believe learned counsel in this case is Mr. Dapo Oladapo Davies."

"Then why is he not here? That's what I want to know," His Worship said, with a trace of judicial anger in his voice.

"Most probably something to do with the publication in the press about the visit of the Chief Justice to the prisons and the directive that certain cases be transferred to the High Court."

"I too have read that in the papers," His Worship announced. "But if learned counsel resort to taking instructions from the pages of newspapers, I do not. Till I receive definite instructions in writing from the office of the Chief Registrar to the contrary, all cases listed in my court will proceed as before."

"As Your Worship pleases," the friend of court observed.

"And any counsel that fails to turn up for his case for the untenable reason that he has read something in the press or heard something on the radio will face the consequences of his error of judgment."

"As Your Worship pleases."

After writing something for what looked like a long time, His Worship looked up to ask the man from the office of the DPP what date he would like the case adjourned to. After a consultation of diaries on both sides, the case was adjourned to a date three and a half weeks ahead.

When shortly before that date I went to remind our lawyer about it, he told me a more serious though interesting story. Three days before that time, a friend had told him that the case had been called at Court 2, at the Mainland High Court. Apparently, the case had been transferred there, even though the relevant court papers had not reached our lawyer. A learned colleague had stood in for him and asked for an adjournment to 13 April 1976. Unfortunately, that date was not convenient for him as he was due to address the court at Island Court No. 4 that same day. His junior would, however, be there. He already had instructions to ask for an adjournment to any of three alternative dates already given him, which would be suitable for both the judge and the State Counsel.

It all surprised me. First, the confusion in the whole judicial system. One would have thought that, as in heaven, order would be the first law in the judicial system. Here, lack of coordination between the Higher and the Lower Benches had now resulted in both handling the same case at the same time. Confusion in place of order. The irony of it all! It was not so long before that time that we were begging everybody that was anybody of importance to prevail on the slow-moving system to get the case started in one of the courts. Now that it had eventually reached the High Court and the judge was ready to hear it, someone else was not ready—our own lawyer!

"Can't you make some other arrangement to enable you to start the case on 13 April instead of asking for an adjournment?" I pleaded with Oladapo Davies.

"Impossible." That was his laconic answer.

"What worries me is the fact that every adjournment means so many more days for our men in prison custody," I pleaded.

"Yes, I know," he said, unfeelingly. "My junior will be in court that day. He will ask for a date not far ahead. I hope both the Judge and the State Counsel will cooperate."

We put the time made available by the two adjournments to good use by mending our fences. First, I took Emmanuel Ojerinde to our lawyer. The man had remained faithful to his promise to be our witness and to tell the truth. I had no doubt that we too were keeping our side of the bargain. Sooner or later, Erebor would be asking me for money.

"Where's Mr. Oladapo Davies?" I asked the clerk at the reception room on the second-floor chambers of Dapo Oladapo Davies at Denton Street, one of the flats in a block of six which the owner had converted into offices for lawyers, accountants, and businessmen in the boom that had suddenly come to the property market.

"Not in," the clerk said most sullenly.

I was by now used to the sullen attitude of clerks, receptionists, and salesmen. I was, therefore, not unduly upset. What disturbed me, however, was the absence of the lawyer himself. Yet we had together fixed this appointment three days before. Also, I had reminded him of it that morning.

"When is he likely to be in?" I asked the young man.

"I don't know."

"You don't know? When does he come in the evenings?"

"He can come in any time. You know he is a lawyer."

"Of course I know he's a lawyer. But what is the implication of this?" I asked the boy angrily.

"That means he can come in any time. And he can go out any time."

Most disappointed, I told the clerk: "When he comes, tell him that Banjo has called." I indicated to Ojerinde that we should depart.

"Oho! So you are Mr. Banjo?" the clerk asked.

"Yes. Why?"

"Because Mr. Oladapo Davies said that if you come you should see his junior."

"But why didn't you tell me that before now?" I asked.

"That was what you should have found out first," Ojerinde confirmed.

"But did I know you are Mr. Banjo?" the clerk asked insolently.

"Don't be rude," I exclaimed. I had now completely lost my temper. "Did you ask me my name?"

"Look at this Oga now," the boy said to both Ojerinde and two other people around—the type you see hanging round lawyers' places.

"What's the matter?" someone cried from a room two doors away. A moment after, the owner of the voice came out. I recognized him as the junior. "Good evening, sir," he greeted me. I acknowledged his greeting by a mere nod of my head. I was very angry and could not trust myself to say anything sensible at that moment.

"He asked for Mr. Oladapo Davies, and I told him that Mr. Oladapo Davies was not in. Then he..."

"How many times must you, boy, be told that you must not be rude to visitors?" the junior asked in admonition.

"But was I rude to him? Was I not merely—"

"Shut up," the junior shouted the clerk down in anger. Indeed, I had to appeal to him to keep cool. "Please come in, sir. Please don't be annoyed," he said, leading Ojerinde and me to his room. "It is sad what this country is coming to. Everybody is rude. The clerk. The telephone operator. The police constable. The salesgirl at Kingsway. All rude."

We lamented the shortcomings of this category of officials in Nigeria and observed that it was the courtesy and cheerfulness of their counterparts that made life more pleasant in the more advanced countries of the world.

I was disappointed that it was he and not Oladapo Davies himself who was going to take Ojerinde through his drill. He was going to be our star witness, the only other person besides Jonathan, Paul, and Mrs. Palmer to say that he saw that good-for-nothing Gilbert boy wield the weapon that killed his mother. But perhaps I was expecting too much of a lawyer's services. Presumably, a junior is quite adequate to record the statement of a witness. No doubt the senior would go through it and personally take Ojerinde through it before he actually put him in the witness box. I hoped it would be Oladapo Davies who would do the exercise with Mrs. Palmer.

As Ojerinde and I drove back in my car, I wondered why the police had not sought him and forced him to make a statement. Even though he had fled 22 Fasanya Street when the police raided the place, surely they knew of him and should have made arrangements to find him wherever he might be. Surely this would not be too much for an efficient police force. Of course, they would plead the usual difficulties. Inadequate resources. Lack of cooperation from the public. I heard that they pay a number of informers from a certain vote. I was wondering why they couldn't set one of these informers on Ojerinde's trail. Presumably, that vote, like most votes, had run out! Whatever the cause, the police leaving Ojerinde alone was to our distinct advantage.

For some reason difficult to understand, Belo insisted that we try to get M.A. Natural to change his mind. When I told him that M.A. Natural was determined not to come forward to give evidence, he still insisted that we visit him. Quite obviously a useless exercise, for nothing would make M.A. Natural, the pastor's warden of St. Nicholas Church, come forward to speak the truth. So I showed a lack of enthusiasm about going to him, and Belo saw this. Besides, I thought we should be satisfied now that Mrs. Palmer would give evidence on our side.

One morning not long after this, M.A. Natural himself came to Belo's office at a time that I happened to be there. In fact, I had been discussing with him the fees of Oladapo Davies and was about to go when Belo's secretary announced Martin Abiola.

"You are here too, Kola? Good," he said when he saw me as he came in. "Then I am killing two birds with one stone."

"M.A. Natural," Belo sounded delighted.

"That's me," the visitor panted.

"M.A. Natural," again Belo called him by the name he loved to hear himself called.

"Look, I want you two to vote for me. That's why I've come. And I want you boys to come to the club more frequently. You should have been at the guest night last Friday."

"Was it interesting?" I asked.

"Interesting? Man, you should have been there to see everybody dancing away his cares. Even Bolade Abrahams. If you saw the way in which he was dancing to the music of Emperor Dan Fodio. Really."

"You mean Magistrate Abrahams?" Belo asked.

"Chief Magistrate Bolade Abrahams of the Lagos Judiciary, if you please. The fellow just forgot everything about his being a magistrate and executed the most suggestive figures with the women with whom he danced."

"What were the figures suggestive of?" Belo teased him.

"Bed, of course," M.A. Natural answered promptly. "I had thought that judges and magistrates were above that sort of thing."

"Aren't judges men?" I asked.

"Bolade Abrahams was too much of a man last Friday night. In fact, he got me terribly worried the way he was dancing with Sissy Bintu."

"Oh yes?" Belo said.

"If my missis wasn't there with me, I would have walked up to him and taken Sissy Bintu away from him. But my missis was there. You see my trouble," the man said, laughing at himself. We all laughed.

"Now I want you two to vote for me. I'm standing for vice-president at the elections. We need some sanity in the place. I want all my friends to support me."

"Easy win for M.A. Natural," Belo said. "M.A. Natural, VP."

"That's me," M.A. acknowledged, taking a cigarette from the pack Belo offered him.

"Yes? Yes? Who's it?" Belo was now speaking to the receiver of his intercom. Neither M.A. Natural nor I had heard the thing ring. Must be one of these fancy ones with silent bells. "I see. No, I'm busy now. You know what? I'll see him for a minute out there in the corridor. You two will have to excuse me for a moment," he said, dropping the intercom. He got up and stopped in front of a chest of drawers. He took out what looked like a pocket calculator before going out.

After Belo returned, M.A. Natural came back to the subject of the Mainland Club elections. "I'm serious about standing. I hope you two will come. That's the first thing. And then vote for me, which is more important still."

"Easy win for M.A. Natural," again Belo teased. "But something I've been wanting to ask you, M.A. Nat. Seriously."

"Yes?"

"This thing about your being at the murder scene at Sissy Bintu's. Kola here is upset that you won't come forward..."

"Look, man, I've told Kola the truth. You see, all three of us are boys. And we all do what boys do."

"No, I don't know what you are referring to," Belo said. "What exactly do boys do?"

"Who are you deceiving?" M.A. Natural became serious. "What about Lara? What about that Calabar woman? And..."

"No. I don't know what you are talking about. For me, it's one man, one wife," Belo said blandly.

"That's just the point," M.A. Natural took off again. "I just will not do anything that will make me get into trouble with my one wife. Nothing whatsoever."

"You mean Sade does not know about Sissy Bintu?" Belo asked.

"Why do you think she doesn't know? She's just being a sensible woman, my friend."

"No, she doesn't. And Kola wants me to go to the police to say that I was at Sissy Bintu's and that I saw the fight and the man that wielded an axe handle on the night of the fight. How can I?"

"But is it true? That's the point," Belo asked.

"True? Of course it is true. Of course it is true that the hemp-smoking boy used an axe handle. We, that is, Sissy Bintu and I, saw it all from her room. Sitting-room, I mean," he explained when Belo's face lit up as he contemplated what else must have been going on in Sissy Bintu's room that night. "The boy wielded the thing backwards above his head, to get momentum, before striking your man—what d'you call his name?" here he turned to me.

"Jonathan. Jonathan Egbor," I said.

"Yes. It was Jonathan he wanted to strike. No, not him," he corrected himself, "the man's son. Wielding the axe handle backwards over his head, so the thing hit this woman on the head. I hear the woman was his own mother."

"So that's how it happened?" Belo asked.

"That was how it happened. And I have told Kola so. But I'm sorry, I'm not going to say that to the police. I know that's what Kola wants. Whatever I do, Sade must not know that I visited Sissy Bintu that day or any other day. I respect my wife. And there's my position in the church too. I cannot afford to face any scandal. That's the truth."

"But you know that because of your stand, Jonathan Egbor and his son are in custody. And they may be hanged," I said, appealing once more to his sense of justice.

"Look, Kola, I know how you feel. But I will not do anything that will give the game away to my wife. I can't."

"I can now understand M.A. Natural," Belo said.

"You can?" I asked, amazed.

"Thank you, man," M.A. Natural said. "We are all rascals. Boys will be boys."

"Yes, boys will be boys," Belo repeated, laughing. I remained silent.

"The sanctity of the home and keeping it intact must take priority over everything else," M.A. Natural said philosophically.

Two days later, the standard of behaviour of magistrates and judges was once more the centre of gossip in my office. Both Belo and Superintendent Dada were with me.

"You should have seen Chief Magistrate Bolade Abrahams at the guest night last Friday. He just forgot completely everything about being a magistrate. He enjoyed himself thoroughly,"

Dada confirmed what M.A. Natural had told us two days before.

"And the following day, he once again became God Almighty," I said in derision. "Your Worship. Your Lordship. As your Worship pleases. You must not cough. That would be contempt of court. If you sneeze—"

"Hold it, man. Not as bad as that," Belo said.

"I am sick at the hypocrisy of the whole performance," I declared.

"What my wife and the other women were saying about Chief Magistrate Abrahams and judges generally at the guest night was most embarrassing and uncomplimentary," Dada said.

"There you are," I said, pleased at Dada's support.

"But what can they do?" Belo asked. "They are men before they are judges. And above all, they are Nigerians."

"Very true, very true," I said. "You are not suggesting, though, that in other countries judges are not men?" I asked.

"I don't mean that they are women—or that they have been castrated," Belo explained.

"Good Lord, castrate Bolade?" Dada cried, laughing. "Why, half the socialites of Lagos will take anyone who did that to court for damages."

"To his court," I cried, and all of us laughed at the joke.

"Now, talking about castration, I have seen pictures of judges in a book," Dada said seriously. "I mean judges in Britain. I think they are a cross between true paintings and caricatures—you know, artists' impressions. What impressed me most in them is the air of detachment and serenity about the judge. The English judge appears to stand completely apart from all worldly pursuits—wealth, women, houses. They give the impression that they are not interested in any of these things."

"That is the true picture of the judge abroad," Belo confirmed. "You can see a number of paintings of judges in the Chief Justices' Chambers in the High Court. Those who are called to the Higher Bench abroad are men who in legal learning and experience, both at the Bar or the Lower Bench, in integrity and maturity, are found to be capable of discharging the very onerous and delicate duties required in the office of a judge."

We both of us looked at him. It was obvious he knew his subject.

"Here, the acquisition of wealth continues to be the main preoccupation of the average Nigerian. Most judges, like most lawyers in private practice, doctors, engineers, and accountants, are first-generation educated men. With them, education has been acquired not for its own sake but as a tool for obtaining a position from which money can be made to secure for themselves, their immediate and extended family, a decent standard of living today, and an insurance for the education and insulation of their children from poverty tomorrow. A good number of them come from homes where as children they knew poverty. Judge or no judge, they will see to it that their own children are insured against poverty tomorrow."

"Explaining no doubt the participation of judges and magistrates in the scramble for land in Virginia Bay and other new housing development areas in the new state capitals," I put in.

"Nigerian judges are Nigerians first and then judges after. And don't condemn them. Why condemn them? All of us are Nigerians first, then doctors, engineers, and accountants next. We are Nigerians first, and church priests next. And as Nigerians first, we first go about making both our today and our tomorrow financially assured, before thinking of fulfilling the requirements of the office in which we function today."

"The solution appears simple to me," I declared. I had listened seriously to Belo's analysis. And so had SP Dada. "Let us start from the premise that we do not have in our society enough men who have the attributes required for the high office of judge."

"Wrong, very wrong," Dada said, interrupting me before I had even started. "What I mean is this, sir," he continued, realizing quickly I was once his prefect at school. "I think we have a few men who could answer those requirements. But they don't want to become judges because in their private law practice, they make a great deal more money than the salary they would be paid as judges. Imagine what people like Detomi Williams get from their retainers with the oil companies and the banks. So they don't want to become judges and subject themselves to the discipline and harshness of the life of a judge."

"But aren't we saying the same thing?" I asked.

"Yes, you are," Belo said, seeing the fault in Dada's argument. "The very thing that makes Detomi Williams prefer the fat retainers in his private practice to carrying out the essential duties of a judge, where his assets in learning and maturity would immediately become available to the nation, is what makes us say that we do not have the men we need," I said emphatically.

"Depends on which way you look at it," Dada said. "What you mean is that we have the men but they don't want to serve in the offices in which they are most needed by the state."

The intercom buzzed.

"I don't want to be disturbed by anyone now," I spoke to the receiver. "I'm very busy."

"Yes, sir," my secretary said, understanding.

"What I'm saying is this: The judges and magistrates that we have now, and will continue to have in the next generation, are the products of the Nigerian society of yesterday and of today. They are like you and me, and M.A. Natural, men who must be comfortable and must make their families comfortable today—and tomorrow. They are, like you and me, and M.A. Natural, Nigerian males who like their women, both the one wife at home and the other woman in the rented flat outside..."

"Indeed, indeed," Dada said, laughing. We joined in the laughter.

"You are saying that we should realize the judges and the magistrates are not the recluses of the British Judiciary. They are not going to be angels from God's heaven," Dada continued.

"Exactly," I said.

"And so?" Dada looked at me, afraid to draw the obvious conclusion.

"You are suggesting we should recognize these limitations and reduce the privileges and traditional honour given them?" Belo asked.

"I think so. All this fetish about contempt of court, I think, it's too much. Let us honour our judge. But by God, do not let us continue to worship him as if he is Jesus Christ here on earth. He is not. He is no more than another Nigerian."

After some time, Belo said slowly: "No. You cannot do that. The institution of the judiciary is what we worship, not the incumbent of the office. We must continue to worship through the incumbent the institution behind him. You see what I mean?"

"I do," I said, sadly.

"Not to do that, my friend, will..."

"Amount to contempt of court," I said. We all laughed.

Later that night, I considered another slightly different aspect of the matter: the philosophy behind the adoption of the British legal system and its transplantation to a climate and a culture completely alien to its home origin. An example of the ridiculous way the thing is working out, to my mind, was the way that the imported system completely barred anyone but the witness in the box from speaking in court. However outrageous the lie the witness might be telling in the box, no one—not even the man in the dock who might be adversely affected by the false evidence—must speak out of turn. To do such a thing was abominable in the eyes of the imported legal system.

In the African indigenous court system, however, it was most usual for the man in the dock to shout that the witness in the box was lying, and even to shout that the judge was wrong. "That is your own judgment, and I tell you I don't accept it," a litigant would invariably shout even at the judge. It was not unusual for both sides to a case before the court and the witness and even the judge in a customary court to engage in a shouting session that could last for minutes before the shouts of "Order, Order" from the police constable restored peace of some sort. Yet in this shouting session, the experienced judge can always determine who is telling the truth and who is not. It is sad that the British system imported into the country completely eliminates this truth-establishing mechanism built into the indigenous judicial system.

FIFTEEN

We mustered in strength at Mainland Court No. 2 on 13 April 1976. I knew, of course, that the case was not really going to start that day, thanks to our lawyer who had said that he would not be able to come to court. Our people, like myself, thought that a miracle might happen and he might be able to come and the case might start after all. So we all came, in large numbers: the family, relatives, townsmen and friends of Jonathan Egbor. But unfortunately, no miracle happened. Our lawyer was not in court.

"Case No. MCJ 31/76/D/Lagos State versus Jonathan Egbor and Paul Egbor," the clerk announced. As Jonathan and Paul hurried to the dock, I pondered the upgrading in the status of the case. In the Magistrates' Court, it was Commissioner of Police versus Jonathan Egbor and Paul Egbor. Now it was not the Commissioner of Police but the whole of Lagos State that now stood against this helpless, innocent citizen and his equally helpless and innocent son.

The recital of the charge was preceded by a statement by the clerk that the court had been informed by the Director of Public Prosecutions on behalf of the state that Jonathan Egbor was

185

charged with the offence of murder. He then proceeded to the formal charge:

"You, Jonathan Egbor, on or about the 28th day of January 1975, at Surulere, in the Mainland Judicial Division of the State, murdered one Marian Bassey, female, and you therefore committed an offence punishable under section 319 (1) of the Criminal Code. Are you guilty or not guilty?"

"No. I did not kill Marian Bassey. I am not guilty at all," Jonathan cried from the dock, shaking his head. Good old Jonathan. The charge against Paul was similarly read. And Paul also pleaded not guilty. The clerk announced the plea of each of them to the Judge, who appeared to make copious notes in his book.

"My Lord, I appear for the prosecution. My name is Stephen Longson Macaulay," the State Counsel announced. He was long in name and long in stature. After the Judge had again made note of this in his book, he looked up.

"My Lord, I am Olawale Ibidapo, from the chambers of Mr. Dapo Oladapo Davies," the junior to our lawyer announced.

"Where is he? That's what I want to know," the Judge announced from his exalted position on the dais. He looked very impressive and awe-inspiring in the red hood he wore on top of his black robe. That red outfit was an indication that he was presiding over a murder case—an awful reminder that the blood of Jonathan and that of his son Paul might flow at the end of the trial, if they were found guilty and convicted.

"My Lord, he is not here today. We..."

"Why is he not here?"

"We have to address court at Island Court No. 4 this morning. That was an appointment that was fixed before knowledge of the present case came to us. We are very sorry, Your Lordship."

"I see," His Lordship started writing again in his book. I looked at the junior, still on his feet. He too had started using the judicial "we." It usually referred to the client with whom the lawyer identified himself. In this particular case, it obviously meant Dapo Oladapo Davies alone.

"The complaint used to be that the DPP was not ready," the Judge observed. "Now the DPP is ready, but defence counsel is not. Meanwhile, these two people there are suffering in prison custody. They are suffering, you know. How long have they been in custody? How long?"

Junior didn't know how long. I knew: fourteen months, sixteen days. I would have said it. But I must not. I must not say the truth which neither of them knew. I must not. If I did, I would be held for contempt of court. Even though I would be helping them with needed information, I would still be committing an offence. Punishable by imprisonment. This strange judicial system!

After consultations all round, it pleased His Lordship to fix the next hearing of the case for 11 May, exactly four weeks from then.

"As Your Lordship pleases," both counsel chanted in unison at the announcement of the new date.

On 11 May, we were again all there at the Mainland Court No. 2. And what was more important, Dapo Oladapo Davies was there. Our case was No. 4 on the list. So, willing or not, we had to sit through the other three cases.

The first of the cases involved three youths, who were shepherded into the dock. They did not understand a word of English—they were said to be immigrants from Togo. So they did not understand the charge and therefore could not plead guilty or not guilty. Eventually, someone in the establishment of the court who was half-Yoruba and half-Togolese was brought. He helped the court solve the problem of the three youths in the dock. They had no lawyer. They obviously could not afford a lawyer. They would, in all probability, go to gaol for the offence of burglary for which they had been charged, and would have gladly gone to gaol if they were asked directly their choice. But according to the imported British system of justice, the Judge wanted a lawyer to defend them. And if they could not pay for a lawyer, then the State could be made to provide a lawyer to defend them at its own expense. Then, after that, the Judge could gaol them if they were found guilty, and they most probably would. Then they would be a charge on the State for the next nine months or so. The Judge instructed the State Counsel to arrange a counsel for their defence. He then fixed a new date for the next hearing of the case.

The next case was one of criminal abortion. Two men were in the dock: a bearded young man with receding hair said to be a medical doctor in the Mainland General Hospital. The other was short and fat. He wore an expensive lace agbada and showed ample evidence of being a representative of the new class of businessmen who went on overseas trips once every two months.

The young doctor was charged with the criminal abortion which resulted in the death of a woman of nineteen, and of dumping the body in the bush somewhere at the Oregun Industrial Estate. The businessman was accused of aiding and abetting in the crime.

The prosecution was not ready in the case— two vital witnesses were not present in court. Much as they had tried, they just could not get these two witnesses into court yet, the State Counsel announced. He pleaded with the Judge for yet another adjournment. Apparently, there had been adjournments in the past. The defence counsel urged the Judge to strike off the case against his clients. He said that one was a very busy medical practitioner, a young man who had been living under an insufferable cloud for seven months since the police wrongly arrested him. He had since been interdicted on half-pay, causing considerable hardship to him, his wife and four children, not to mention the hardship to his extended family whom he had to support financially. Here was a man in a field in which Nigeria was in very short supply, a man ready to work in the field of relieving human suffering and pain, and of saving life. Ironically, however, he was prevented from doing this since the police brought the charge against him. The other accused person was a businessman whose business had been badly affected by the charge. Both men were ready to go on and to show the court that the charge against them was totally unjustified.

The Judge raised one or two technical points with both the State Counsel and the defence counsel. Then he announced his decision to adjourn the case to a new date mutually acceptable to both counsel.

The defence counsel, however, prayed the Judge to grant bail for both men, as they were both responsible men who would not jump bail. "Your Lordship has the power to grant bail in these circumstances," the counsel asserted.

"Tell me just one section of the Criminal Code that gives me the power to grant bail to a person charged with criminal abortion and who subsequently dumped the body of the abortion victim in a swamp," the Judge said, looking at the defence counsel with displeasure.

"Your Lordship, your powers are wide. Very wide indeed."

"I know that."

"Your Lordship has the power to grant these accused persons bail. You can even..."

"Under which section of the Criminal Code? That's what I want to know," His Lordship was not going to succumb to flattery. The counsel failed to persuade him to grant bail to the accused persons. So he ordered them to be remanded in prison custody. As the men were led away from the dock, I wondered how each of them felt: the fat man whose moment of passion had resulted in an unwanted and fatal pregnancy, and the young doctor who for a fee of a mere fifty, hundred or perhaps three hundred naira had committed a crime which had now landed him in court and would probably earn him a three-year gaol sentence and the destruction of an otherwise bright medical career.

The third case involved accused persons that were not in court. It was conducted in a technical language between the Judge, the State Counsel and a defence counsel who stammered much. I thought he was in the wrong profession. But then he most probably was succeeding, if he had come this far in the profession.

Then the case of Lagos State versus Jonathan Egbor and Paul Egbor was called. But Jonathan and Paul were not in the courtroom. They were probably downstairs. If so, why had they not been brought up? A police officer ran downstairs to go and find out what was happening to the accused persons. On his return, he whispered something to the clerk, who relayed the message in another whisper to His Lordship's ear.

"I hear the accused persons in the next case are not yet here," His Lordship announced. "So we will have a short adjournment."

His Lordship rose. We all rose, the men of the learned profession first, followed by those of us who were not. His Lordship bowed, nearly double. We all bowed, in deference to His Lordship, the Judge. This is the ritual that must be gone through every time the Judge comes in or goes out. He bows. Everyone bows. For he is a very important person. That is why every time he comes in, or goes out, people go through the ritual of rising and bowing.

It was at 11:35 am that the Judge ordered the short adjournment. At 12 noon, the accused persons still had not come. At 1 pm, there was still no news of the Black Maria. At 2 pm, still nothing doing.

Both the lawyers and the rest of us had become restless about the delay in the arrival of the accused persons. A short while after this, there was the usual heavy knocking on the door leading to the Judge's chambers. The lawyers ran back and stood up like schoolboys who had been playing pranks, quickly readjusting themselves in class at the approach of the form master. We all rose in our places. For the big man was about to come in.

He did, with graceful, dignified steps. He turned at right angles to face the court when he reached his seat. He bowed. We all bowed. He took his seat, and we all sat. We must not sit till he had sat first. If anyone sat before the Judge had sat in his own seat, that would be disrespectful to the Judge. Everybody must respect him because he was the Judge. Anyone who failed to respect him would be held for contempt of court, and he would be punished severely.

His Lordship then announced that the case could not go on because the police had failed to produce the accused persons. Why, His Lordship did not know. What His Lordship did know and say, however, was that the police not bringing the accused persons was a serious thing. His Lordship was getting upset by various acts of inefficiency by the police. These acts of inefficiency were affecting the work of the court adversely. Something had to be done about it.

His Lordship rose. We all rose. His Lordship bowed, a dignified, judicial bow. We all bowed. His Lordship retreated in dignified steps to his chambers. We all started to chatter and to disperse.

Out in the corridor, we heard the fantastic story of why the police had failed to produce the accused persons. Apparently, in the police's prison transport arrangement, one "Black Maria" van was detailed to collect from the prison all the accused persons due to appear in court on a particular day. The van then went from court to court distributing its passengers at the appropriate courts. In the afternoon, the van started on the return journey collecting its load of accused persons from the various courts to return them to the prison.

The day before we went to court and the Black Maria failed to turn up, there was a serious hitch in the transport routine. The Magistrate in one of the courts had forgotten to sign some document which would authorize the prison authorities to receive back into prison custody the batch of accused persons whose case had been taken at that particular court that day. Since these men had been signed out of prison custody earlier in the day, the prison authorities refused to admit them back into prison custody without the appropriate warrant duly signed by the magistrate.

The police officer in charge of the accused persons who had been refused re-admission to prison custody then took his human cargo in the Black Maria in search of the magistrate who had forgotten to sign the warrant. He could not be found. The men were then taken to the Central CID headquarters. Even there, the authorities

194

refused to accommodate them for the night. They were next taken to the national headquarters of the police on the Island. Here, some senior official used his initiative to break the chain of bureaucracy. He gave the accused persons admission—quite obviously against set procedure, but he braved it.

By now it was past midnight. And as the police officer in charge of the whole operation had not been able to go through certain other routines that he ought to have gone through in the evening of the day that his charge had been refused re-entry into the Island Prison, the Black Maria, its driver and the police officer himself were just not available to fulfil their scheduled assignment for the following day. That was what happened.

When I told the story to my friend, Superintendent of Police Dada, he thought the whole thing was unfortunate but understandable. "Where accused persons are concerned, the security drill just has to be followed absolutely," he told me. We were at tennis together.

"But surely there must be an allowance for emergencies such as the one which occurred in this particular case," I told him.

"Presumably so. But no one would like to take chances," he said, following the exciting game going on at Court 3. A young school-leaver had taken on one of the club's stars. We watched from the pavilion.

"Who now would bear responsibility for what happened yesterday?" I asked bitterly, remembering that whoever did, the terrible thing had caused Jonathan and Paul so many more days in prison custody.

"That police officer who took an unsigned remand warrant back without checking whether or not it had been properly signed by the magistrate. I suppose everyone would at once put the blame on him," Dada said, warming up. "Nobody would think of blaming the magistrate—oh, that's a good stroke!"

So it was. A fine volley from the youth that completely beat his older opponent.

"Of course the Magistrate must share in the blame," I said. I knew the line he was taking.

"Oh no, no one would think of blaming His Worship. Much too important to be blamed. It is the wretched police officer that must be blamed. We get the blame all the time."

"I suppose it is hard on the police—ah, the boy has been caught there," I cried as the older man first lured his opponent to the net before sending a ball crashing beyond the reach of his arm. It just landed on the base line behind the boy.

"I suppose if our man was an 'A' Levels chap, quick on the uptake, he could have remembered to check the warrant before he left the court. But unfortunately, he was not an 'A' Levels man and he was not quick on the uptake. Those who have 'A' Levels, and those who are quick on the uptake—where are they? You know where they are, sir?" There was a ring of dejection in Dada's voice. "They don't want to come to the police force. Their fathers won't allow them to come to the police force. They go to the universities. They come out as graduates—doctors, lawyers, engineers. They look down upon the police force."

"But I know some graduates come into the force directly now. I met the son of a friend..."

"Oh yes, a few of them do come. Very few. And the mistake is made of taking them on at a level where they don't have the experience of going through the ranks. They are made to race through to the top, doing mostly administration in air-conditioned offices at headquarters. They don't understand the problems and traditions of the force. They in fact cause more trouble than they do good, these graduates in the force."

"Really?"

"Yes. These young men who are taken on directly as ASP and made SP after a short in-service training—what do they know about the suffering of the poor police inspector who, after fifteen years in the service, still has no accommodation and with his wife and seven children still lives in a broken-down Bedford van in the barracks?"

"As bad as that?" I asked.

"Or the inspector in Gongola State who cannot even get a hut to himself alone? And yet it is part of the conditions of service that all rank and file of the force must live in barracks so that they can be prepared for emergencies at all times."

"I see."

"Look, let us watch the game. For I could go on and on. When people blame everything that goes wrong on the police, do they ever pause to find out the terrible conditions under which the police operate? Do they?"

On my way home, I thought of the many problems of the police. They are overwhelming but unfortunately, they are little known to the public.

SIXTEEN

The case opened effectively on 18 May 1976, at about midday, when the prosecution put their first witness in the box. He was Bassey Etim Bassey, the husband of the deceased, Marian Bassey. He swore to speak the truth, the whole truth, and nothing but the truth. After the preliminaries about his full name, where he lived, and what work he did, the State Counsel asked him:

"You knew the late Marian Bassey?"

"Yes. She was my wife."

"Where is she now?"

"Where she is?" Bassey Etim Bassey looked at the State Counsel, puzzled.

"Yes, where is your wife Marian Bassey now? Is she at home at 22 Fasanya Street? Is she in this court? Or has she travelled? Tell this honourable court where she is now," the State Counsel amplified his question.

"My wife Marian Bassey is dead," the man in the witness box said slowly and sadly.

"Your wife Marian Bassey is dead," the State Counsel repeated, writing in his book.

"Murdered. Murdered by this man and his son..."

"No, no, no," the State Counsel cried.

"Mr. Bassey, I must warn you to limit yourself to answering the questions counsel puts to you," the Judge cut in disapprovingly. He appeared angry with the witness.

"You must not say things you are not asked, Mr. Bassey," the counsel, too, warned him. "You are not competent to say who killed your wife. This is for His Lordship to determine after listening to your own evidence and the evidence of the other witnesses who will come to testify in this court."

"What is the witness's answer to your question, Mr. Macaulay?" the Judge asked.

"The witness said that his wife is dead, my Lord," the State Counsel replied.

Thereafter, the Judge wrote down something in his book. So did the State Counsel in his book. And so did our own lawyer, Dapo Oladapo Davies, as well as his junior. The Judge and all the lawyers appearing on both sides of the case all wrote down things in their books. They were endlessly writing down things in their books. And they took a long time about it.

"Yes," the Judge looked up, a signal that the State Counsel could proceed with his examination of the witness.

"Were you at home when your wife died?"

"At home? I was not at home. If I was at home, do you think I would have allowed that man and his son to kill my wife?" the witness asked belligerently, pointing a finger of anger at Jonathan and Paul in the dock.

"I must again warn you to answer the questions put to you, Mr. Bassey," the State Counsel said with some anxiety. "You must leave this honourable court to decide whether or not your wife was killed. And if so, who killed her. Now answer my question: were you at home when your wife died?"

"No. I was not at home."

"Tell this honourable court..." The State Counsel did not complete the instruction. He noticed that the Judge was still writing. He himself started writing in his own notebook. Our lawyer Oladapo Davies and his junior were both writing too.

After the Judge had looked up, the State Counsel repeated the unfinished instruction. "Tell His Lordship how you came to know that your wife had died."

The witness in the box looked at the Judge for some time. From the Judge, he turned to the State Counsel. Then he looked at Jonathan and Paul in the dock, and he appeared angry again. But after counsel had again requested him to tell how he came to know of his wife's death, he said:

"That Friday, I went to work. I was on afternoon duty. So I left home at about one o'clock. I did not come back till about 10 pm."

"Where exactly did you go to work?" His Lordship asked.

"At Ikeja. I work in the Nigerian Textile Mills. That's where I went, leaving my wife at home."

The Judge, the State Counsel, our own lawyer, and his assistant all started to write again. Apparently, that question the judge asked about where Bassey worked was important. And therefore all these important men stopped to record the reply of the witness to it.

"Yes," the Judge said, looking up.

"I think you said that you came back from work at about 10 pm," the State Counsel reminded the witness.

"I came back at about 10 pm. When I came back, my brother's wife and my daughter told me that there had been a big fight in the house."

"What is the name of your brother's wife?"

"Her name is Elizabeth."

"You must tell this honourable court the surname of your brother's wife."

"My brother's wife's surname? She is Elizabeth," the witness said emphatically.

"Elizabeth is her Christian name," the counsel explained. "What we now want is the surname. She's Elizabeth what?"

"What?" the witness asked, confused.

"Alright. What's your brother's name?" counsel asked.

"My brother's name? His name is Joseph Akpan. That is my brother's name."

"Your own name is Bassey—Bassey Etim Bassey," His Lordship observed. "That other man's name is Joseph Akpan. Yet the two of you are brothers. Ask this man in the witness box," the Judge now addressed the State Counsel, "ask him: is this a case of true blood brother relationship or just the usual story of distant kinship?"

After some persistence on the part of the State Counsel, the explanation eventually came out that Bassey and Akpan came from the same hometown near Calabar, and so belonged to the same patriotic union. There the relationship ended. Again, all the important men wrote down this important information.

Bassey then went on to describe how he had first gone to the Mainland Police Station No. 2 to look for his wife, as he had been told that she had gone to that police station. When he got there, he said he was told that his wife was not there, but that she had gone to the Mainland General Hospital for treatment. He then took a taxi to go and look for his wife at the General Hospital.

"And who did you see when you got to the General Hospital?" the State Counsel asked.

"When I got to the General Hospital, I saw my son Patrick and my daughter Clara. They were crying."

"Did you ask them why they were crying?"

"Yes, I did. They just continued to cry. Then my brother told me to come to the place where my wife was in the hospital."

Again they wrote, all the important people. Throughout the narration of this painful story, these important people—the Judge and the lawyers—wrote and wrote and wrote. And because they spent a long time writing, I dozed off in my seat.

"So you saw your wife, Mr. Bassey?" the State Counsel's voice woke me.

"Yes. I saw her."

"Did she say anything—did she say anything to you, Mr. Bassey?"

"But she was dead. How could she say anything, when she had been murdered by that man and his son?"

"Mr. Bassey, your wife was dead. That was the important thing that you discovered in the hospital," the State Counsel said, writing. Again, they all wrote, led by the Judge.

"Then when you had discovered that your wife had died, what did you do?"

"What could I do?"

"I mean, did you stay in the hospital? Or did you go home to sleep?"

"Sleep? If your own wife died like that, can you go home to sleep?"

"My friend Mr. Bassey, you must answer questions put to you," the Judge cut in angrily. "You must not ask counsel questions. You see, we are all sorry about the personal tragedy that you have suffered in the unfortunate death of your wife. But I have allowed you plenty of latitude for this tragedy. You must, however, not take undue advantage of this to insult counsel in my court. You will therefore answer questions as they are put to you. Is that clear?" the Judge asked.

The man in the witness box was silent.

"Do you understand my question?" again the Judge asked.

"Your Honour, I understand," he muttered.

"Counsel should ask the question again."

"When you discovered that your wife had died in the hospital, did you go back home to sleep?"

"I went back home. But I could not sleep."

Much writing all round.

"What happened the following day?"

"What happened?"

"Yes, what happened? Did you go anywhere the following day?"

"I went somewhere. I went with the police to the mortuary. They asked me if the dead woman was my wife. I told them that... that... that the dead woman was my wife," the witness said, sobbing.

"You identified the dead woman at the mortuary as your wife," the State Counsel put the answer in more technical language, as they all wrote.

"Yes, I identified her as my wife."

"And where is she now?" the State Counsel asked, as an afterthought.

"Where she is?"

"Yes, where is she now?" the State Counsel asked again, his voice indicating anxiety that the witness might at this tail end of his evidence again say something that might anger the Judge.

"We have buried her."

"You have buried her. Where?"

"In my hometown."

"Where is your hometown?"

"Oron, Cross River State."

"Oron, Cross River State," the State Counsel repeated, writing. He then checked through his notebook, leaf by leaf. Then he looked up suddenly, and asked:

"Mr. Bassey, after you had identified your late wife at the mortuary, did anything happen that day? At the police station?"

"Yes, something happened at the police station."

"Tell His Lordship what happened at the police station."

"I made a statement at the police station."

"You made a statement at the police station. Would this be the statement you made at the police station, Mr. Bassey? Please show the witness this," the State Counsel addressed the clerk, handing him a sheet he detached from his file. This the clerk handed to the witness. "Look at it. Is that your signature at the bottom?"

"Yes," Bassey said after examining the document.

"And is the document in your writing?"

"Yes."

"So that is the statement you made to the police?"

"Yes."

"My Lord, I seek permission to tender this document."

After another round of writing all round, during which the document in evidence had been passed first to our counsel and next to the Judge, who examined it and scribbled something on it, he announced: "This document will be admitted as Exhibit D."

"As your Lordship pleases," the State Counsel replied. "And that will be all for this witness."

The Judge announced a short break. It was welcome all round. For everybody was tired: the Judge, the State Counsel, our own lawyers—they all looked tired after all the writing. Writing, writing, writing. I wondered why they did not tape-record the evidence of the witnesses in a case. I thought that this would be making the fruits of modern electronics come to the aid of justice by speeding it up. But the Judge and the lawyers chose to write everything down in longhand. And if you asked them why they were writing down everything in longhand, you might be committing a contempt of court. And then you would be in trouble with the Judge.

After the Judge had come back and everyone had taken his seat, it was Dapo Oladapo Davies' turn to question the witness. Adjusting his blue gown, he asked:

"Mr. Bassey, you and the first accused have lived together at 22 Fasanya Street for a number of years. Is that not so?"

"Yes," the witness answered after some hesitation.

"During that time, has there ever been any quarrelling or fighting between the two of you?"

"No," again the witness answered guardedly.

"In other words, you have been living amicably together as co-tenants?"

"Yes."

"Yes, you have been living amicably together," the lawyer repeated slowly, writing. Again, they all went through the ritual of writing.

"And Mr. Bassey, you were not at home at the time of the alleged fight, is that not so?"

"I was not at home. But my people were at home. My people told me what happened."

"You yourself were not at home, Mr. Bassey?"

"I was not at home."

"Therefore, you did not see the fight?"

"No. But people..."

"People who were at home told you of the fight. You yourself did not see the fight. Or did you see the fight?" Dapo Oladapo Davies repeated the question, looking at Bassey in the witness box.

"I did not see the fight myself," Bassey said with the reluctance of a man convinced that the statement he was being forced to make would certainly affect his case badly.

"And all you have told the court is therefore hearsay."

"My Lord, I object to the way my learned friend is conducting his cross-examination," the State Counsel cried, springing to his feet.

"Alright then, to please my learned friend I'll put my question in another way," Oladapo Davies said. "All the things you have told this honourable court are things which you heard other people say to you?"

"Yes."

"Yes. That will be all, my Lord."

I was a bit surprised. I thought that our lawyer would ask Mr. Bassey more questions than he did. Just what were we paying all the tat tees for? Presumably, the importance and value of a cross-examination lay not in the length but in the quality of it. I sincerely hoped so. While what Dapo Oladapo Davies asked Bassey Etim Bassey was important, there were many other things that he ought to have asked the man. How I wished I was a lawyer. I would have asked that man so many questions that the Judge and everybody would know that he and the other people behind him had no case against Jonathan and Paul. Sadly, I was no lawyer!

SEVENTEEN

Barrister Oladapo Davies finished the cross-examination of Bassey Etim Bassey, the first witness, at 2:40 pm. The man had, in all, been nearly three hours in the witness box. I thought in my mind that all the evidence he gave could have been given in a matter of forty to sixty minutes if the Judge had not had to write down his evidence in longhand in his notebook.

At 2:40 pm, I was hungry. I had thought that the end of the evidence of the first witness was the point where the Judge would conveniently call it a day. But he did not. Rather, he asked that the second prosecution witness be called in.

"I see Your Lordship intends to continue," the State Counsel observed.

"Yes, I do, Mr. Macaulay. What about you?"

"Since it is rather hot and we have no electricity and therefore no air-conditioner working..."

"With or without NEPA's co-operation, or in spite of NEPA's failures, I intend to continue sitting. And you, Mr. Macaulay?"

"We follow where Your Lordship leads," the State Counsel said.

"Your Lordship's constitution and industry are a household word in the circle of learned friends," Dapo Oladapo Davies rose to participate in the debate to continue or not to continue.

"I see he is perspiring," the Judge indicated with his judicial hand the State Counsel. "But what is he wearing that makes him perspire? That flimsy gown. But look at me. Look at me. See what I am wearing..."

We all looked at him and his long scarlet gown and silvery wig, a combination that one could have described as ludicrous in a court in tropical Africa but for the fact that he was a judge. To even suggest that anything about a judge was ridiculous was to be guilty of contempt of court.

"I too am hot," the Judge continued, mopping his face with a clean pink handkerchief which he brought out from the deeper reaches of his robes. "I thought that Your Lordship should not be exposed to excessive hunger, noting that Your Lordship has had only one cup of tea since morning."

"Thank you, Mr. Macaulay. I wasn't aware that learned counsel these days see through closed doors, since neither you nor Mr. Oladapo Davies was in my chambers at 11:30 am to see whether I had one cup of tea or two of cocoa."

The lawyers laughed at the humour of the Judge. The Judge himself laughed. But few of us in the body of the court laughed. What brought us to that court was not funny. We wanted them to get on with the case so that the two dear people in the dock might be released quickly.

"I appreciate the concern you have for me, Mr. Macaulay. All the same, we will call in the next witness."

"As Your Lordship pleases."

She was a woman in cheap green lace and no jewellery whatsoever. She had a baby strapped to her back. She did not speak English but understood Yoruba. The preliminary ritual of recording her name, where she lived, and what she did for a living was somewhat tedious after the relatively smooth oath. She called the first prosecution witness her husband.

"Mr. Bassey Etim Bassey is your husband, you say?" the State Counsel, Macaulay, asked her.

"Yes."

"But you said earlier on that the name of your husband was Joseph. Joseph Akpan."

"Yes."

"Did she say yes to that question?" the Judge asked. "Ask her then which of her two husbands is the father of the baby strapped to her back. Ask her," the Judge said.

The lawyers laughed at the mischief behind the Judge's question. We in the inferior portion of the court giggled and hurriedly smothered the giggling. We were afraid. When the interpreter had interpreted into Yoruba what the Judge had said, the woman said in justifiable anger: "Everybody knows that my husband is the father of my child Clara. How can the father of my husband be the father of my child? Do people do this kind of thing in this part of the country?"

Our lawyer, Dapo Oladapo Davies, then sought leave of the court to explain the woman's predicament. She was apparently caught in the web of extended family relationships. The evidence of the first prosecution witness, whom the witness now in the box first called her husband and later her husband's father, indicated that this woman's husband was merely a townsman of Bassey Etim Bassey.

"I see," the Judge observed, implying that he saw what every one of us that was not learned had seen before all this meaningless, needless argument. "To this woman, every male member of the extended family of her husband and every townsman of her husband is also her husband, according to native law and custom."

"Thank you, Mr. Oladapo Davies. You may now proceed, Mr. Macaulay."

"Mrs. Akpan, you were at home in the evening of 28 January 1975?"

No reply from the woman in the dock. She shuffled from one leg to another, trying to placate the baby on her back. That worthy had woken up and was showing the first signs of protest against the strange atmosphere to which it was being exposed.

"I repeat the question. Mrs. Akpan, were you at home, or were you not, at 22 Fasanya Street, Surulere, on the evening of 28 January 1975?"

"I don't know which day was 28 January 1975. So I cannot tell you that I was at home that day."

"Alright. Were you at home the day there was a big fight in your house?"

"You mean the day that Papa Paul and his son killed Mamma Edna? I was at home that day if that was the day you mean."

"Mrs. Akpan, you must listen carefully to my question and answer just what I ask you," the State Counsel cried, forestalling the Judge's intervention. "All I want to know at this stage is: were you at home that day, or were you not?"

"That day when they fought in our compound, you mean?"

"Yes, that day people fought in your compound."

"I first went to market to sell rice. Then I came back."

"Yes. What happened after you came back?"

"Papa Paul and his son fought with Mamma Edna. They killed..."

"Mrs. Akpan," Macaulay cut her short sharply, before she blundered too far again into the forbidden region. "Who is Papa Paul?"

"There he is, standing there," she pointed to Jonathan in the dock.

"And who is Paul?"

"Papa Paul's son. That one standing near his father," she said, shuffling from one leg to another. The baby on her back continued to cry in a muffled voice.

"And who was Mamma Edna? Was she the wife of the first prosecution witness?"

She looked at Macaulay blankly.

"Was Mamma Edna the wife of Bassey Etim Bassey?"

"Yes."

"What happened during the fight?"

"Papa Paul's son took an axe handle and hit Mamma Edna."

"But did the man just get hold of an axe handle and begin to smite the woman without anything going on before? No preliminary exchange of words? Ask her, Mr. Macaulay, ask her," the Judge ordered.

"The Judge wants to know what happened before the second accused hit Mamma Edna. Tell the court why the second accused hit Mamma Edna."

The woman in the witness box suddenly decided that her baby was more important than all of them—the lawyer asking her questions, Jonathan and Paul in the dock, and even the Judge. In a lightning movement, she transferred the baby from her back to her left side where she held it with her left arm. She still had enough movement of that left hand, which she used in collaboration with the free right hand, to undo some zip in her upper underwear above the left breast. This she brought out and, completely unmindful of the several pairs of eyes, including the Judge's, staring at her, she proceeded to suckle the baby on the breast.

Everyone was silent. No one dared laugh at what obviously some of us could have found funny in a non-court atmosphere. There was anxiety clearly written on the face of Macaulay, the State Counsel. But the Judge put everyone at ease.

"Let her carry on. It's a natural function, the instinct of a mother to cater for her child first. Let her carry on," the Judge ordered.

She carried on at her own pace, and the pace of the baby happily tugging at and greedily sucking the fount of its nutrition, completely regardless of the number of men and women staring at her, and completely regardless of what they thought of her action. After finishing the first and longer half of this natural operation, she withdrew the tit of the breast from the tiny mouth of the infant, who did not protest, put the breast back under her upper underwear, and proceeded to suckle the baby on the other breast. After a good draw down on the milk in this other breast, she removed her baby from it and proceeded to put it back on her back.

"Mrs. Akpan," Macaulay called her back to the unpleasant duty that had occasioned her presence in the court in the first instance. "What did Mamma Edna do to Jonathan Egbor and Paul Egbor before Paul Egbor attacked her with an axe handle?"

"Paul was fighting with Edna. And Mamma Edna told Paul to stop fighting with Edna. But Paul did not stop fighting with Edna. So Mamma Edna abused Paul. Paul was angry. He held the axe handle. He hit Mamma Edna with the axe handle. And..."

"Wait a moment, wait a moment," Macaulay said, as he noticed that the Judge had started writing down what the witness had been saying. They all, that is the three lawyers, followed where the Judge had led. It had been quite a mouthful; what the witness had said, via the interpreter, had taken a long time.

"Then what happened?" the State Counsel asked, waking me up from a short nap.

"Blood came out of the nose of Mamma Edna."

"Blood came out of the nose of Mamma Edna," Macaulay repeated, writing.

"And after that?"

"I went to call my husband's brother."

"What happened after you came back?"

"When I came back, I could not find Mamma Edna. She had gone to the police station. From the police station she went..."

"Wait a minute. You came back and did not find Mrs. Bassey, or Mamma Edna, not so?"

"It is so. She had gone to the police station."

"You mean you were told that she had gone to the police station. You did not see her go, did you?"

"How could I see her if I had gone to call my husband's brother?" She adjusted the baby on her back.

"Did you go to see her at the police station?"

"But she had left the police station for the hospital."

"Look, ask her where next she saw the deceased woman," the Judge ordered impatiently. "Ask her."

"Where next did you see her?"

"But she had died," she said belligerently. "How could I see her after she had died? Is it a pleasant thing to see a ghost?"

"Did you see her dead body?" Macaulay asked.

"No."

"You never saw her again, alive?"

"No. She was dead. We all saw the coffin."

"My Lord, that will be all," Macaulay said, sinking down in his chair.

After the Judge had been writing for some time, he looked up with a slight wrinkle creasing the exalted face. "Didn't this witness make any statement to the police, Mr. Macaulay?" he asked.

"Oh, my Lord, she did," Macaulay replied, a little disturbed.

"Don't you want to put the statement in evidence, then?"

"My Lord," Macaulay said, leafing through his papers for the document. "Ah, here it is. Now Mrs. Akpan, did you make a statement to the police? When the police took you to the police station, did you say anything to them?"

No reply from the witness in the box. She adjusted the child on her back.

"Did the policeman ask you some questions at the police station? Look at this paper. Show it to her," Macaulay handed the document to the clerk for onward transmission to her. "Is that the paper the policeman wrote down when you were talking to him?"

The woman looked at the document with suspicion. She said nothing.

"This witness cannot read or write. So you cannot expect her to tell whether or not that was the statement she made to the police," the Judge said, a little cross with Macaulay. "Read it to her, and interpret it. Then she can say whether or not that was her statement. Read it to her."

The clerk read it, interpreting it sentence by sentence:

My name is Elizabeth Akpan. I live at 22 Fasanya Street, Surulere. I live with my husband at the above address. I was at home on 28 January 1975. I saw the beginning of the fight between Papa Paul and Mamma Edna. Mamma Edna is the wife of Mr. Bassey. When both Papa Paul and his son began to fight with Mamma Edna, I went out of the house to go and call my husband's brother. When I came back, I heard that Mamma Edna had gone to the police station. I did not see anyone hold an axe handle during the fight. This was all the thing that I saw during the fight. Mamma Edna has now died. I did not see who hit her with axe handle. This is all I know about the case.

"Is that what you told the police?" Macaulay asked the witness.

"That is what I told the police."

"My Lord, I seek to tender this," Macaulay said, indicating to the clerk to take it from the witness. He passed it first to Oladapo Davies and then to the Judge, who, after writing something on it, announced: "This document will be admitted as Exhibit E."

"As your Lordship pleases," Macaulay said mechanically.

After writing for some time, the Judge looked up. "What is the time now?" he asked.

All counsel began scanning their wristwatches. So did the clerk.

"I make it 3:30, your Lordship," Dapo Oladapo Davies said, rising to his feet.

"3:30. Do you wish to cross-examine the witness today, Mr. Oladapo Davies?"

"I will, if Your Lordship is not too tired to continue. My cross-examination will not take more than twenty minutes. I will ask witness only two questions."

"Good. Proceed, Mr. Oladapo Davies," the Judge ordered, writing in his book. Again the three lawyers wrote in their books.

"Mrs. Elizabeth Akpan, you and the late Mrs. Marian Bassey were close relatives by marriage?"

No reply.

"Were you and the late Mrs. Bassey close relatives by marriage?" Oladapo Davies repeated the question.

"Yes."

"And you are sad that she has died. Are you not?"

"Why would I not be sad? Was she not my senior?"

"She was your senior. This makes you sad that she has died. And you would like to see punished whoever you were told was responsible for her death, not so?"

"Yes."

Macaulay made a movement as if he wanted to say something. But he did not.

"You remember the statement you made to the police, Exhibit E. In that statement, you said that you went out at the beginning of the fight. When you came back, Mrs. Bassey—er—Mamma Edna, had left the house for the police station. Not so?"

No reply.

"Do you understand my question?"

Still no reply.

"I must warn witness that she must answer counsel's questions," the Judge intervened.

"When you came back from where you went, Mamma Edna had left the house, not so?"

"Yes."

"Therefore, you were out when the second accused, that is Paul Egbor, was alleged to have hit the deceased Mamma Edna with an axe handle?"

"I was at home."

"But you heard read to you a few minutes ago the statement you made to the police. In that statement, you said that you saw the beginning of the fight only. You went out to go and call your husband's brother immediately after the fight began. When you came back, you heard that Mamma Edna had gone to the police station. And listen carefully. You said to the police that you did not see anyone hold an axe handle during the fight. That was all you had seen. You saw no one hit the late Mamma Edna with an axe handle. That was your statement to the police. Is it not?"

"It is what I told the police," she said.

"But is that not the truth, that you saw no one hit Marian Bassey with any weapon? Was it not the truth that you told the police?"

No reply.

226

"Alright then, Mrs. Akpan, did you see anyone hit Marian Bassey with any weapon?"

"Yes," witness muttered.

"Then what you told the police in that statement is not true, Mrs. Akpan. You either lied to the police, or you are now lying to this honourable court. Which is it?" Oladapo Davies asked in a menacing tone.

No reply.

The Judge fixed the witness with a stony stare and said: "Woman, I hope you understand what counsel has said. Do you agree that either what you told the police in your statement or what you have been telling me, and all what you have been telling all of us today, are lies? Do you understand that?"

The woman opened her mouth, and then closed it.

"Do you admit that either what you told the police or what you have been telling me today is all lies?" again the Judge asked.

"But is it not God that has put you in this important position and made you so big that people have to tell lies before you?" the woman asked seriously.

"Really!" the Judge exclaimed, a reaction which immediately drowned the giggling that the witness's reply had evoked. After regarding her for some time, the Judge turned to Oladapo Davies: "Any more questions, Mr. Oladapo Davies?"

"Yes, m'Lord. Now Mrs. Akpan, I want you to tell the truth this time. You see, I am not in an important position. And I am not big enough for people to lie before me."

Here the court roared with laughter.

"Mrs. Akpan, when the late Marian Bassey had fallen, what did you hear her say?"

No reply.

"Did you, or did you not, hear her say 'Gilbert has killed me, Gilbert—'"

"Objection, my Lord," Macaulay roared, jumping to his feet.

"Witness will answer counsel's question," the Judge ruled. Macaulay sat down, wounded.

"'Gilbert has killed me, Gilbert has killed me.' Did you hear the late Marian Bassey say those words, where she lay helpless on the concrete floor?" Oladapo Davies asked again, slowly.

The witness shook her head and adjusted the baby on her back.

"I take this to mean that your reply to my question is no. Now to my next and final question to you, Mrs. Akpan. I again remind you that I am not in an important position. You therefore need not tell any lies before me. When the late Marian Bassey had fallen on the concrete floor moaning, 'Gilbert has killed me, Gilbert has killed me', what did you say?"

"Nothing," witness muttered.

"Are you sure you said nothing?"

"I am sure."

"Did you not say: 'Gilbert done kill 'im mother'?"

"No. I said nothing."

"But you saw Marian Bassey fall. And you heard her say 'Gilbert has killed me, Gilbert has killed me'."

Silence in the witness box.

"Elizabeth Akpan," Oladapo Davies said slowly, bending forward slightly. "I put it to you that neither in your statement to the police nor in your evidence in the witness box today have you spoken the truth."

No reply.

"I put it to you that you lied in your statement to the police that you did not see anyone wield the axe that hit the late Marian Bassey. I put it to you that you, in fact, saw Gilbert Bassey hold the axe handle that felled the late Marian Bassey. I put it to you that you heard her say the words 'Gilbert has killed me, Gilbert has killed me'. And

I put it to you that you yourself shouted the words: 'Gilbert done kill 'im mother'."

No reply. Witness adjusted the baby on her back.

"I put it to you that, in this instance, you told a lie to the police that you saw nothing because you were afraid of the police."

"I was afraid. We were all afraid," the woman said, shrugging her shoulders.

"Yes, you were afraid. You were afraid of the police. Everybody is afraid of the police," Oladapo Davies said slowly. He paused for a moment. He then continued: "I put it to you, Elizabeth Akpan, that the story you have today told in this court—that you saw Paul Egbor hold an axe handle with which he hit the late Marian Bassey—is not true. I put it to you that it was in fact Gilbert Bassey you saw hold the axe handle with which he hit his mother—accidentally. And I put it to you that you have come to tell this falsehood today out of a misplaced loyalty to and sympathy for your relative-in-law, Bassey Etim Bassey. That will be all, m'Lord."

"Any re-examination, Mr. Macaulay?" the Judge asked, looking up after he had written a great deal in his book.

"Just one question, my Lord. Mrs. Akpan, I want you to cast your mind back to the events of that day when there was a fight in your compound. Listen carefully. Answer truthfully. Did you see anyone hold an axe handle that day?"

"Yes," the woman muttered.

"Who held the axe handle that day?"

"That one," she said, pointing in the direction of the dock.

"Which of them, father or son?"

"Son."

"You mean Paul Egbor?"

"Yes."

"Did anyone hit the late Marian Bassey with the axe handle?"

"Yes."

"Who?"

"That one."

"Which one, father or son?"

"Son."

"You mean the second accused, Paul Egbor?"

No reply.

"You mean Paul Egbor."

"Yes," she said scarcely beyond a whisper.

"That will be all, my Lord."

EIGHTEEN

The trial did not resume until a fortnight later. We were told that this was due to the Judge being indisposed after the marathon session which had lasted until near 5 pm on the first day. There had been admiration from all of us for the way the Judge had pressed on with the case on that occasion, in spite of the indications that counsel on both sides were tired and exhausted. What was done that day—going through the evidence of Bassey Etim Bassey and the longer evidence of Elizabeth Akpan, which was made trebly tedious by the need for interpreting from English to Yoruba, or the other way round, before being recorded in longhand by the Judge in his book, could easily have taken two or three days at the normal pace of work in the court.

The court started with the evidence of Police Inspector Mohammed Shitta. Led by the prosecuting State Counsel, he went through the usual preliminaries of stating his name, rank, and his current posting. He was in charge of this and three other cases at the Central CID on the Island. What this meant was that the police officer who did the physical investigation worked under his supervision. He had himself since been transferred from Lagos to Gongola State, and it was from there that he had come to give evidence. He was shown the statements made by Bassey Etim Bassey, Elizabeth Akpan, Gilbert Bassey, Jonathan, and Paul Egbor. He admitted having seen all the statements and identified the signature of Corporal Samuel Akinsan, who had signed either as the recorder of the statement or witness to the statement in each case.

"You did not yourself investigate this case, Inspector Shitta?" Dapo Oladapo Davies opened the cross-examination.

"I supervised the investigation."

"You did not yourself visit 22 Fasanya Street, Inspector Shitta?"

"It was not necessary, since Corporal Akinsan had visited the place."

"You will answer my question directly, Inspector Shitta. Did you yourself visit 22 Fasanya Street or not?"

"I did not."

The Judge led the counsel on both sides in the ritual of writing down both the question and the answer.

"You yourself did not see any weapon which could have caused the death of the deceased woman, Marian Bassey, did you?"

"I did not."

"Nor did you recover personally from either the first accused or the second accused persons any murder weapon, or did you?"

"No, I did not."

"This will be all, my Lord."

After the Judge had been writing in his book for quite a while, he looked up at the State Counsel and asked: "Mr. Macaulay, I fail to see the point of this witness's evidence. How much has this man's evidence advanced your case?"

After some hesitation, the State Counsel replied cautiously: "The prosecution is in some difficulty, my Lord."

"The prosecution is always in difficulty, I know. But what's your difficulty this time, Mr. Macaulay?" the Judge asked, looking at him.

"We've been encountering considerable difficulty in getting hold of Corporal Samuel Akinsan, Your Lordship. Police headquarters told us he was in Kwara State. They helped us radio the Kwara State Police Commissioner. We at first had information that the witness had been contacted, and that he would be here today."

"But he is not here now," the Judge said tersely. "What story do they have to tell now? They are always having one story or the other to tell. Yes, no one can beat the police when it comes to telling stories."

There was smothered laughter in the rank of learned friends. But we in the body of the court dared not laugh.

"They scatter their officers all over the country," Macaulay observed. "And when we want them, they can no longer be re-assembled. Transferring officers frequently is the trouble with the police, my Lord."

"Yes, we know. But they don't want the police to feel too comfortable in one place," the Judge commented. "The Inspector-General wants to keep them on the move. That keeps them from mischief, eh?" and the Judge laughed. They all laughed, in apparent understanding of what he meant. We too understood what he meant and laughed guardedly.

"What the prosecution in effect is saying is that since the police officer who did the actual investigation is not available, the next superior officer will do," the Judge remarked. "Am I right, Mr. Macaulay?"

"Your Lordship is always right, my Lord."

"Half a loaf is better than no bread, Mr. Macaulay?"

"It is an old adage, my Lord." The other lawyers laughed at the wit of both the judge and their colleague.

"Yes. But I'm afraid I don't see any nutrition whatsoever in your half loaf this time," the Judge observed. "Even a most inexperienced junior at the Bar would see the worthlessness of the evidence of the last witness. The man did not personally investigate the case. He did not personally take down any of the statements. Now you bring him here to come and waste the time of the court. It is, of course, your case, so carry on as you please."

I was glad that things were going badly with the prosecution. Gilbert Bassey was the next witness called by the prosecution. We exchanged glances in our ranks as he followed the police orderly into the courtroom. We knew that the moment he opened his accursed mouth, lies, and nothing but lies, would issue from it. And true to our prediction, he started by telling a blatant lie. He said he did not understand English! Imagine that scoundrel saying that he did not understand English.

"Not even Pidgin English?" the Judge asked, surprised. The wretch in the witness box shook his head. Yet the Judge's question was asked in English!

Proceedings were adjourned for some time to enable the court officials to find someone who spoke Efik. The Judge took advantage of the break to go for tea. We went downstairs for some biscuits and soft drinks.

The tedious process of going through the preliminaries of name, address, and occupation was made more tedious after the resumption of proceedings by the difficulty the witness was experiencing in his attempt at keeping up the pretence that he did not understand English.

"What is your occupation?" the State Counsel asked the routine question.

"I am an applicant," Gilbert Bassey said in near-perfect English. We all laughed in spite of ourselves.

"What is that?" the Judge asked.

"Applicant, Your Worship," the man who did not understand English said, without waiting for the interpreter to first render the question in Efik.

There was spontaneous laughter in court. Even we joined in the laughter.

"Applicant! What profession is that?" His Lordship asked to know, turning to Mr. Macaulay.

"The witness means, Your Lordship, that he has written a number of applications to government offices seeking employment. He is still waiting for the results of these applications," Macaulay explained.

"I see," the Judge observed. "These people have upgraded the status of the search for employment in offices to a profession. Presumably, the University of Lagos will soon be awarding a degree in this new discipline."

Again, there was general laughter. And again, we all joined in it. After a few more routine questions, the State Counsel asked Gilbert Bassey to state in his own words his own account of the events of the fateful day at 22 Fasanya Street, Surulere.

The witness said that on that day he came home early, after checking on his applications in the Ministries of Education, Agriculture, and Works, as well as in BP and John Holt in Lagos. When he came home, he found that Paul Egbor and his father were abusing his mother. When he told them not to abuse his mother, Paul Egbor started to abuse him. When he told Paul to stop abusing him, Paul went into his father's room and brought out the handle of an axe.

"This is a hot lie, very bad lie," Jonathan Egbor shouted from the dock. "All what—"

"Mr. Egbor, you must not speak from the dock," the State Counsel, Macaulay, shouted at him.

"But the man is telling terrible lies," Jonathan Egbor again shouted from the dock, agitated. "How can I keep quiet when the man is lying against me?"

"Now, you are here to follow the official procedure of court, Mr. Egbor," the State Counsel warned. "You are not to speak unless you are put in the witness box over there. And you are not to shout at counsel or at anyone else, as you do in your customary court. You must understand. And you are not to interrupt this or any other witness."

Jonathan was surprised. He looked disappointedly at his lawyer, Oladapo Davies. He no doubt was shocked to see the man we were paying to defend him keep quiet instead of supporting him on this fundamental point. He shrugged his shoulders.

Oladapo Davies rose slowly and said, "I apologize to Your Lordship for the unbecoming behaviour of my client. I assure Your Lordship that it was not intentional and that it will not happen again."

"That is alright, Mr. Oladapo Davies," the Judge said. "Accused persons will have the opportunity of telling their own versions of the case when they get into the witness box. Until that time, they must not interrupt the evidence of the witness in the box. Witness may now proceed."

I watched the disappointment in Jonathan's face. But what could I do, or what could anyone else do to help him?

Gilbert Bassey continued his evidence. He said that when his mother saw Paul with the axe handle, she begged Paul not to hit him with the weapon. Paul was very annoyed. So he ran after his mother and hit her with the axe handle. And his mother fell.

Jonathan Egbor opened his mouth but closed it again. Irrespective of the magnitude of the lie, he must say nothing from the dock. That was what the judge and his own lawyer had said. So he must keep quiet.

"Did your late mother, Marian Bassey, provoke the second accused before he hit her with the axe handle?" the State Counsel asked.

"No, Your Honour," the witness answered, without first waiting for the interpreter to render this in Efik. I whispered to the man next to me my hope that the Judge would take note of this, that Gilbert Bassey understood English very well.

"And what did you do then, after the second accused had hit your mother with the axe handle?"

"I asked his father to see what his son had done to my mother."

"Did you fight him then?"

"No. I never fought him. I never fought them."

After a few more questions to which Gilbert Bassey gave false answers, the State Counsel announced that he had concluded the examination-in-chief of the witness. Dapo Oladapo Davies then rose to open the cross-examination.

"You told this honourable court that you are an applicant, Mr. Gilbert Bassey?"

"Yes, sir," he answered. He did not wait for the interpreter.

"Did you pass the West African School Certificate?"

"I sat the examination, sir."

"Did you fail the examination?"

No reply.

"Answer my question. Did you fail the West African School Certificate Examination?"

"I did not pass, sir."

"You started the examination. Did you complete it?"

No reply.

"Were you, or were you not, sent out of the examination room for cheating?"

No reply.

"I must warn the witness that he must answer counsel's questions," the Judge ordered.

"Were you not sent out of the examination room for cheating, Gilbert Bassey?"

"The invigilator wanted to put me in trouble," Gilbert Bassey said excitedly. I sat up in my seat. Things were becoming interesting.

"Why? Why did he want to put you in trouble?"

"I don't know."

"You don't know? You know alright. I put it to you that you were sent out of the examination room because you cheated, as you have always cheated and lied all your life."

"I do not tell lies. I don't cheat."

After allowing the Judge to complete recording that part of his cross-examination, Oladapo Davies continued: "Gilbert Bassey, do you or do you not understand English?"

Again, no reply. The interpreter, on his own initiative, started to interpret the question into Efik. But Oladapo Davies cried like a wounded lion, ordering the interpreter to stop the operation. He then asked again loudly: "Gilbert Bassey, remember you are on oath. Gilbert Bassey, school certificate attempted, do you or do you not understand English?"

"I understand small."

"You understand small. Enough to have answered in English many of the questions already put to you today in English, without the interpreter first interpreting."

No reply.

"I put it to you that you have been lying to this court when you pretended not to understand English."

"I understand small."

I adjusted myself in my seat. We looked round at ourselves in satisfaction. Our lawyer was earning his pay. After the usual round of writing, Oladapo Davies continued:

"Gilbert Bassey, do you know Indian hemp?"

"My Lord, I object to the line the cross-examination of my learned friend is taking," the State Counsel shot up.

"If my learned friend objects to my question, I will ask it in a different way, my Lord. Gilbert Bassey, do you know the effect of Indian hemp?"

"It is not good."

"It is not good. You know it is not good. How do you know that—"

"My Lord, I object to the way my learned friend is trying to insinuate—"

"Again, my Lord, as I see that my learned friend is so anxious to shield his witness in this particular aspect, I am willing to forego the reference to Indian hemp at this stage. But I may come back to the point to show that certain actions and behaviour of the witness are very similar to the actions and behaviour of persons addicted to the weed. So I may come back to the point."

"You may proceed," the Judge ordered.

"Now, Gilbert Bassey, I want you to tell the truth this time."

"My Lord, I object to the ..."

"My Lord, I object to the frequent interruptions of my learned friend," Oladapo Davies angrily stopped his opponent from completing his objection. "These two men, father and son, are being tried for murder. Father and son are in jeopardy of their lives. We have every right under the law to conduct the defence in an atmosphere free from unnecessary interruption and harassment from the prosecution."

The two counsels sat down. The Judge said nothing for a while. He was apparently allowing tempers to cool. We looked around at the audience. We were obviously getting something for the money we were paying Oladapo Davies. We were thrilled by his performance.

"Counsel may proceed," the Judge eventually ordered.

"Most obliged for your usual consideration, m'Lord," our lawyer said urbanely. "Now, Gilbert Bassey, what did your mother say after you had felled her with the axe handle?"

"My Lord, I must again register my objection to my learned friend's putting words into the mouth of the witness."

"Right, I'll put my question in a different way. Gilbert Bassey, what did your mother say

245

after she had fallen down, after she had been hit with an axe handle?"

"I did not hear her say anything."

"'Gilbert has killed me! Gilbert has killed me!'" Oladapo Davies said in a thin female voice. "That was what your mother, the deceased Marian Bassey, said when she fell."

"No, she never said that."

"She never said that. What did she say?"

No reply.

"Tell the court what your late mother said when she fell on the concrete floor, helpless. Tell the court what she said in her agony."

"She said nothing."

"She said nothing? Remember you are on oath. Do you believe in dreams? Are you not now seeing in your dream the ghost of your deceased mother, lying helpless on the concrete floor and moaning: 'Gilbert has killed me! Gilbert has killed me!'"

"My Lord," Macaulay was again on his feet protesting. But the Judge appeared to ignore him.

"And Mr. Bassey, Gilbert Bassey, do you know one Elizabeth Akpan?" Dapo Oladapo Davies asked slowly.

No reply.

246

"Now, Gilbert Bassey, a simple question. Do you or do you not know one Elizabeth Akpan?"

Still no reply.

"Now that you have had enough time to think out the lies you will tell, I ask you for the third time: do you or do you not know Elizabeth Akpan?"

"I know her."

"Who is she?"

No reply.

"Who is Elizabeth Akpan?"

"She is a co-tenant."

"Was she present during the fight between you and the second accused?"

"I don't know."

"Did you hear her say anything after your mother had fallen down?"

"She never said anything."

"But Gilbert Bassey, you only a short while ago said that you did not even know that she was present at the fight between you and the second accused. If you are certain that she did not say anything, then you are lying when you said you did not know that she was present at the fight?"

No reply.

"You are in fact lying now, as you have in fact been lying all through this evidence, Gilbert Bassey?"

"I do not lie," Gilbert Bassey said feebly.

"Did you not hear that woman cry: 'Gilbert done kill 'im mother'? Now for once, tell the truth."

"She never said so."

"She never said what?"

"She never said 'Gilbert done kill 'im mother'."

"What then did she say?"

"I never remember."

"You never remember. She did say something, which you now conveniently do not remember? Try and remember what Elizabeth Akpan said when your mother had fallen down after the blow from the axe handle."

"I never remember."

"You do not remember what Elizabeth Akpan said. But you now remember that she was in fact witness to the fight?"

No reply.

"Gilbert Bassey, I put it to you that when your mother was felled by the weapon wielded by you, she cried out in agony: 'Gilbert has killed me,

Gilbert has killed me'," the lawyer said with emphasis.

"No. She never cried so."

"And I put it to you that when Elizabeth Akpan saw what you had done to your mother, she cried out: 'Gilbert done kill 'im mother'."

"She never said so."

"And I put it to you that all you have been telling this court is one bundle of lies calculated to mislead this court."

"I never tell lies," he said feebly.

"And Gilbert Bassey..."

"Yes, sir," the witness answered to his name.

"You see those two there, father and son?" Dapo Oladapo Davies asked, pointing at Jonathan and Paul.

"Yes, sir," Gilbert Bassey said, looking at Jonathan and Paul. We all joined in looking in the direction of the dock.

"Those two are the wrong ones in the dock," the lawyer said with emphasis, his voice rising. "I put it to you, Gilbert Bassey, school certificate attempted, self-confessed professional applicant, you, and not Jonathan Egbor and his son Paul Egbor, should be there, there in the dock. You should be there in the dock on a charge of manslaughter, for the accidental killing of your own mother, Marian Bassey."

"No, sir," Gilbert Bassey muttered.

"This will be all for this witness, m'Lord," the lawyer said, sinking into his chair, exhausted.

NINETEEN

I was certain it was she. Sissy Bintu. It was the merest fraction of her back view that I saw as she entered the taxi some fifty metres ahead of my car. But I knew it was she. I raced a bit to overtake the taxi before it manoeuvred itself away from the kerb. I pulled to a stop in front of it.

"See dis Oga now," the taxi driver shouted. "If na taxi driver drive so bad de go say taxi driver crazy. Now see how dis big Oga drive so reckless."

"Driver don't vex, I beg you," I said, apologizing to the driver as I came out of my car.

"Oh, it's you, Mr. Banjo," Sissy Bintu exclaimed. She immediately collected her handbag and started coming out of the door I held open for her.

"Madam na so?" the taxi man asked in disappointment at the loss of a ₦2 fare. "Master, how now?"

"That's alright, my friend," I said as I slipped a ₦1 note into his hand.

Sissy Bintu's company was worth a good deal more than ₦1 any day. She had already made herself comfortable in the passenger's seat when I joined her in my car. And the fragrance of her perfume was already pervading the inside of the car.

"And where have you come from, Sissy Bintu?"

"From the lawyer," she said, mopping her left cheek with a dainty blue hanky.

"Which lawyer, if I may ask?"

"Which lawyer, you are asking? Was it not you who arranged that I should see him?" she asked, a little surprised.

"You mean you have come from Dapo Oladapo Davies?" I asked, sharing my attention between the traffic and the conversation. One just had to watch that traffic.

"Of course it is Mr. Oladapo Davies. And I have told him everything I know about the case."

We were both silent for some time. I was disappointed that she had been seeing Dapo Oladapo Davies alone. I was in truth jealous, even though I probably had no justifiable cause to be jealous since she was not my wife. But it was I who did the tedious though pleasant duty of persuading Bintu Palmer to agree to give evidence on our side. The arrangement was that I should take her to see the lawyer whenever he was ready to take her through the rehearsal of her evidence. Now she had been seeing him alone. Dapo Oladapo Davies was much younger than Sissy Bintu. But he was handsome and fast— the type that the Bintus of our society would fall for any day. And Bintu, I thought, could fall for anyone ever so easily.

"He has told you what to do, then?"

"Oh yes, he has. I'm to listen to the question the lawyer asks. I must think carefully before I answer. As if I am a schoolgirl going to give evidence in court for the first time," she hissed. I laughed. She too laughed.

"You are going home, I take it?" I asked her.

"I'm going home. I'm tired," she said, yawning.

Going home, to prepare for the visit of my friend M.A. Natural, most probably going to prepare a meal of rice and fish stew. Or just the fish without the rice. How I envied M.A. Natural. And how I began to dislike our young lawyer. These thoughts raced through my mind. But I still managed to concentrate on the traffic.

"You know something, sir? If not for you, and for Mr. Egbor, I would still refuse to give evidence in this case," she confessed.

"I know, Sissy Bintu. And I appreciate it," I told her, stealing a few seconds off my concentration on the traffic to throw a side glance at her. I put my right hand on her left lap.

"Ah, ah, ah. Where d'you think you are?" she asked, removing my hand from the forbidden region.

"In the car, of course," I said, looking back on the road to be sure that all was still well with the car.

"You know you are on the steering wheel?"

"Of course I do," I told her.

"Then face your steering," she advised, coquettishly. "I don't want trouble. I don't want to die in an accident."

"Nor do I," I confessed.

"Then you must look straight, and not do as if you don't have a wife at home," she said.

I was embarrassed. I took her advice and concentrated on the traffic. She too did the same.

"All you men are the same," she observed after some time.

"In what way?" I asked, looking sideways at her.

"You keep your own wife in a respectable way at home and begin to tamper with other women outside."

"But why d'you say that, Sissy Bintu?"

"See what you are doing now. There's Bola at home. She thinks butter won't melt in the mouth of her husband. But see what you are trying to do to me in the car now."

"Just what am I doing to you, my dear lady?" I asked her, trying to repeat the game.

"Mind, mind that madman," she cried, as a Datsun taxi tried to force me out of my lane. I took her hint. I allowed the madman to have his way. After I had readjusted myself to a safe position behind the taxi, my fair passenger sighed deeply.

"What is it, Sissy Bintu?" I asked her.

"Oh, nothing," she said, sighing again.

"Why are you sighing, then?"

"Just thinking."

"Thinking of what?"

"You," she said simply, and she sighed again.

"I'm flattered. And what are you thinking of me now?" I asked, again trying to adjust myself to the rough motoring all around.

"I want to ask you a question. Can you do for me the things that Nat is doing for me?"

"Do for you the things that M.A. Natural is doing for you?" I repeated the question—a most unexpected question.

"Yes. Can you do for me the things that he is doing for me now?"

"But he is your boyfriend. I am not," I told her, throwing a glance at her.

"That's what I want to hear. You men are all the same. You will want to have an affair with another man's woman. You will not want to share responsibility for her upkeep. Always wanting to reap where you do not sow."

"But Sissy Bintu, are you ready to leave M.A. Natural?" I asked her seriously.

"If I leave Nat, are you prepared to take over?" she asked.

"Of course," I said, putting my right hand on her lap again.

"Oga, face your steering," she said, again removing my hand. "I know you cannot be serious in what you are saying. I'm too old a fish to be caught that way. And besides, Bola is a good woman; I cannot do anything that will wreck her home. So, my dear."

I thought of Sissy Bintu for quite a while after I had dropped her at 22 Fasanya Street. The access was very bad, but I risked the springs of my car in my desire to get my pleasant passenger delivered safely to her doorstep.

Much as I would have desired to have her company in bed, I was impressed by her attitude. While she was content to play the role of the "other woman" in the married life of my friend Martin Abiola, alias M.A. Natural, she kept herself sufficiently behind the scene not to be a nuisance and a bother to Mrs. Abiola. Nor was she loose enough to be picked up by anyone, like me, wanting a diversion from the straight and narrow path of fidelity in wedlock.

Back home, I was surprised to find that my uncle, Papa Ota, was awaiting me. He was, as usual, comfortably seated and snoring softly on one of the deckchairs on the verandah, with his tobacco pipe on the occasional table and his walking stick on the floor.

Raliatu was in the kitchen. That annoyed me. For I had come to know that Papa Ota and Raliatu never came visiting together without some problem, real or imaginary, which the distraught woman would insist on taking to my uncle at Ota instead of coming to us straight. But eventually, my uncle would bring the matter back to us.

This time Raliatu had gone to Papa Ota requesting that he put her on to a moneylender. She needed a sum of ₦40 which she wanted to give partly to the Chief Warder and partly to another two warders at the Island Prison to make them show favours to Jonathan and Paul.

"I thought that she was talking woman's talk at first," my uncle said when he woke up. "If we needed to spend money this way, my son Kola knows when and on whom to spend such money. That was what I told myself. But then this woman was crying very much. I told her to go and see you. That was what I told her. But she said you would not listen to her. And..."

"But Papa Ota, which person does Raliatu say asked her for money?" I asked impatiently, even though my uncle had mentioned three warders. "Raliatu, tell me now, did these people really ask you for money?" I demanded of her, without waiting for an answer from my uncle.

Raliatu sobbed. That was all she did in these circumstances. Sob, sob, sob.

"Tears won't solve your problem, woman. Who really asked you for money?" I demanded again.

Raliatu now broke down.

"Daddy, how can anyone in Raliatu's state of mind answer the questions you ask?" Bola asked. "And I tell you, this is why Raliatu goes to Papa Ota instead of coming to us here. You don't show sufficient patience with her."

"I see."

"The truth is that Raliatu is afraid to tell you that she needed money to give to the warders. You would consider that to be bribing people to do their work."

"I suppose I would be wrong if I consider it so? I suppose that would not be bribing people to do their work?" I demanded.

"Daddy, you are too rigid in your views," my wife, my lawfully wedded wife, admonished me. "Giving a little amount of money to a warder who has shown favours to Jonathan and Paul is no more than an act of gratitude for such favours."

"My son, I want you to listen to the words of my mouth," my uncle intervened. He was now sitting in one of the armchairs in the sitting room. He removed his pipe from his mouth. "I want you to set about the release of the son of the daughter of the sister of your father the best way you know. That is the thing I want you to do. I have said to myself that my son Kola will not allow the son of the daughter of the sister of his father and his son to die in prison. That was the thing that I said to myself."

"But Papa Ota, Daddy thinks that everyone is like himself," Bola said. "Just because he will take no money from anyone, he thinks that other people don't accept money. I hear it was Jonathan himself who asked Raliatu to bring money for the warders who are helping him and Paul."

"But it is wrong, Bola—it is criminal," I pleaded. "And both Jonathan and Paul may get into greater trouble. Can't you see?"

"My son, we must not do anything that will cause more trouble," Papa Ota said, sucking rapidly at the stem of his pipe. "I do not want you to do what government does not want. But, but it is God that has put the warders in a job where they receive gifts. That is the thing I want you to remember, my son. And the pastor has also said that when people work at the altar of God then they are expected to feed at the altar of God. That is what the pastor said, my son. But I do not want you to do what government does not want, my son. And I know that you will not abandon the son of the daughter of the sister of your father. That is the word of my mouth."

A few days later, I got more information from Jonathan himself. It was during our next visit to him at the Island Prison. On this occasion, Bola and I received VIP treatment, thanks to the intercession of a truly important person. The Chief Warder called Jonathan and Paul out and allowed Bola and me to talk to them in his own office. It was such a difference from the usual arrangement, in which half a dozen visiting relatives of persons in custody in the prison carried on shouted conversations with their relatives lined up on the other side of the hatch in the partition wall separating the warder's office from a corridor in the prison.

"I hope you are well, Jonathan," I asked him.

"I am well, master," he said.

"And you, Paul?"

"I am well, sir," Paul grunted.

Neither of them really looked well. Paul in particular looked bad. His eyes appeared swollen and red.

"You are not well, Paul," Bola confronted him.

"I am well, Mummy," he insisted.

"Master, I cannot deceive you. Paul is not at all well," Jonathan said.

"Why did he not see the doctor yesterday?" the Chief Warder asked.

"The doctor did not come yesterday, master. He came last week."

"But did you report this to the warder on duty?" the Chief Warder asked.

"Report to him? Did he not see that the boy was very sick, and did he do anything? The man merely told me that my trouble was too much and that I was not the only one in prison custody," Jonathan said bitterly.

The prison boss appeared surprised and embarrassed. "But why did you not report this to the senior warder, Mr. Egbor?"

Jonathan did not answer. He merely stared at the floor, tears welling up in his eyes.

"Cases like this must be brought to the notice of the senior officer on duty at once," the Chief Warder told us. He was short and fat, with a badly kept beard. "I will make arrangements for the boy to be taken to the Island Hospital tomorrow."

So saying, the prison boss rolled out of the room, presumably going to set the ball rolling for the visit of Paul to the hospital the following day.

"Master, the things that happen in this place are terrible. I am afraid to talk," Jonathan said after the Chief Warder had left the room.

"What is it, Jonathan?" I asked.

"Those warders, master. They are wicked. Very wicked. If you don't give them money, they don't listen to you. They just treat you in a wicked manner, master."

"But where do they expect you to get money from when you are in custody here?" I asked him.

"But master, the relatives bring the money when they visit us."

"The warders allow the relatives to give the money to the people in custody?"

"Is it not the warders themselves who take the money from the relatives for the inmates?" Jonathan answered with a question.

"What is now important is that Paul must go to the hospital tomorrow," Bola said.

"And master, I want you to beg the Chief Warder to transfer Paul to the same cell where I am. I do not like the place where they put him now."

"You are not in the same cell, then?" I asked.

"No, master. The place where they put him is full of bad people. They are real criminals. They take Indian hemp in the place every time."

"Indian hemp!" I exclaimed. "Where do they get it from?"

"Not the warders themselves sell the thing to them? It is the warders, master. And I fear for Paul. The way I see his eyes so, I think they are already teaching him how to take Indian hemp."

"No," Paul grunted.

"When I told the senior warder to help me transfer Paul to my own cell, he said he will do it. I know it is money he wants, master. But I was afraid to tell you this."

"But Jonathan, you should have told me to talk to the Chief Warder," I told him.

"Master, but the thing is hard. When you go now, and the Chief Warder leaves the office, the senior warder and the other warders will punish me and Paul for talking to the Chief Warder."

"What now shall we do?" I asked helplessly.

"Master, please I know it is bad, but we must give money to them. If we don't give the money to them, we will continue to suffer in this place."

Then the Chief Warder came back, perspiring. "I've arranged that," he panted, sinking into his chair. "Mr. Egbor, you should take your son to Senior Warder Abdulahi tomorrow morning."

"Yes, sir," Jonathan said, looking at Paul.

"He will arrange for two warders to take him and three other inmates to the Island Hospital."

"Yes, sir."

"Most obliged for all this you are doing for Mr. Egbor and his son," I said to the Chief Warder. "I don't know how to express my gratitude."

"Oh, that's alright," the prison boss said. He was still perspiring profusely.

"And just one thing. Is it possible at all that the two of them be kept in the same cell?" I asked as if it was an afterthought.

"Are they not now in the same cell?" the prison official asked. He looked at Jonathan.

"No, sir," Jonathan answered. "Don't you know I am in C1 whereas Paul is in J4?"

"I see, I see. We normally don't put relatives together, but I'll make a note of this request in the book. I'll see what we can do about that."

"I really don't know how to thank you," I said, getting up to go.

"Thank you, sir," Bola said.

"It's a pleasure, Mrs. Banjo," the Chief Warder said, accompanying us to the gate.

TWENTY

Disaster of a major character struck our case two days after the last court hearing. Emmanuel Ojerinde died in a motorcycle accident. He was the man who was going to be the star witness for the defence. He was the man who had at first, like the rest of the occupiers of 22 Fasanya Street, refused to give evidence for fear of being killed. He was the man whom we had to pay just to come forward to speak the truth, the whole truth, and nothing more than the truth. The fear that he might be killed if he gave evidence appeared now to have been well-founded. Even I now believed that his death had something to do with the case in court.

"How did it happen?" I asked Gregory, who came to my house with the terrible story.

"He collided with a Lagos City Transport bus, sir," he said.

"He was riding a motorcycle, you say?"

"Yes, sir. A friend's motorcycle."

"Whose was it?" I asked, as if knowing the owner of the killer machine would bring back Ojerinde to life.

"They say it belonged to one of his co-workers. They say he died before people, rushing him to the Orthopaedic Hospital, got him there."

"My God," I exclaimed.

"Those people are terrible, master."

"I suppose you think Bassey's people are responsible for this?"

"Sure, sir. Those people are terrible."

When I told Belo the story, he confirmed that it was truly a serious disaster which had overtaken our case. He suggested we should again put pressure on both M.A. Natural and Nwanna to come forward to give evidence. They would be necessary, in addition to Bintu.

"Not now that Ojerinde has died after his decision to come forward to give evidence," I said bitterly. "Not one of that lot will have the courage to come forward now. Certainly not Mrs. Palmer."

"I have no doubt that Ojerinde's death will be linked with the case," he said reflectively.

"It is certainly linked with the case, man," I said grimly.

"Of course it is linked—"

"You mean you, too, believe that the two things are connected?"

"Look, how else can you explain Ojerinde's death?"

"Explain Ojerinde's death? Simple. The wretch did not take sufficient precaution. He collided with a crazy LCT bus. You are surprised? Don't you yourself see how these motorcyclists weave in and out of traffic, going from right to left, and from left to right, as if they are exempted from all the rules of the road? Don't you see them riding in the wrong direction on one-way streets? So why are you surprised?"

"Why should it happen to Ojerinde and not to someone else not connected with the case on our side?" I asked stubbornly.

"Who told you that other motorcyclists not connected with our case are not being killed? Have you been to the Orthopaedic Hospital to count them with their shattered limbs? Have you been to the mortuary to see how many of the corpses are motorcycle accident victims? Man, they are being slaughtered and maimed by the dozen on Lagos roads every day."

Three days after this, Belo and I drove to 22 Fasanya Street to plead once more with Nwanna to change his mind and come forward to give evidence for the defence. As we sat in his modestly furnished parlour while a small boy went to call him from the third house, I pondered on the link that connected him and M.A. Natural. Neither of them would come forward to speak the truth they knew. Whereas M.A. Natural's fear was for his marriage, Nwanna's fear was for his life.

After pleasantries, I lied to Nwanna that my friend and I were merely passing by and had called to say hello to him when we saw that his door and windows were open.

"Thank you, sir. How's missis?"

"Missis is alright," I said.

"Is this the house where your friend who's in police custody lived?" Belo asked, pretending not to know much about the case.

"Police custody? Prison custody, not police custody," I corrected him. "Graduated from police custody to prison custody ages ago. The one is very bad. The other is hell."

"Is this the house where I hear Mrs. Palmer lives?" Belo asked.

"Yes, sir, but she's out now," Nwanna answered.

"I see," Belo nodded his head.

"I hear the case is already in court," Nwanna observed.

"Yes, it is," I told him.

"And I hear that the police have really got the wrong men. Is it true someone else killed the woman that died? Was Mr.—er—" Here Belo turned to Nwanna, trying to remember his name.

"Nwanna," I helped him out.

"Was Mr. Nwanna at home the day of the incident?" he asked him.

"Oga, I was at home. I cannot deceive you. Even though I don't have to talk to you, I am not afraid of you. I know you are not a CID man."

"CID man!" Belo repeated. We both looked at each other and laughed.

"What I say is that I know that you are not a CID man. You don't know me but I know you. My brother works under you, and he tells me you are a good man."

"So, it's good to be good," I observed, smiling at Belo.

"Is it true then that it was someone else who wielded the axe? I hear the murder weapon was an axe, or was it a machete?" Belo asked.

After a slight hesitation, Nwanna said: "Yes. It was Gilbert Bassey who carried the axe handle which wounded his mother. I have told Mr. Banjo this."

"But why did the boy do that?" Belo asked.

"Well, it is like this. He went to fetch the axe handle after Paul, that's Mr. Egbor's son, had floored him. He was ashamed that Paul had floored him. Everybody tried to part them. Everybody pleaded with them to let the fight finish there. Then everybody went his way."

"Yes. Then what happened?" Belo asked, showing increasing interest.

"Gilbert Bassey was still angry. So he went to his father's room and brought out the axe handle. He was running after Paul. So Paul's father was trying to stop him. And his own mother was crying that he might accidentally kill somebody with the axe handle. She was holding on to his shirt, trying to stop him. But that boy Gilbert is a crazy man. Every man in this street knows he is a crazy man. Indian hemp. That's what he lives on."

"Is that so?" Belo looked at him keenly.

"Yes. He smokes Indian hemp. He takes drugs. He is a rogue. No work. His papa is even very sad about him."

"So he wanted to smash—er—Mr. Egbor's head?" Again Belo prompted him.

"No. He wanted to kill Paul. So Mr. Egbor was trying to stop him. He wanted to wound Mr. Egbor. As he carried the axe handle up above his head so..." here Nwanna demonstrated it, "the axe handle hit his mother's head."

"The mother was behind him?" I asked, as if hearing the story for the first time.

"She was behind. She was holding on to his shirt. She was begging him not to commit murder. She said government would kill him if he killed any person."

"So that is how it happened," Belo said, with interest. "And the police are holding the wrong people?"

"Yes, sir. It was Gilbert Bassey who killed his mother. Everybody knows it in this house. Even everybody in this street now calls him a murderer."

"I see," Belo observed.

Nwanna looked at my face. He read in it what apparently made him uncomfortable. For he quickly proceeded with saying: "Mr. Banjo wanted me to say all this in my statement to the police. But I cannot. I don't want to die. Who will take care of my children and my mother if I should die now?"

"I see," Belo nodded. "But why should you die if you give evidence, if it is true evidence?"

"Oga, I cannot deceive you. If I give true evidence in this matter, they will kill me. I know them; you don't know them. They will kill me." After a slight pause, he continued: "I pity Mr. Egbor and his son. They are suffering for something they did not do. If our police had done their work properly, they would have discovered that Gilbert Bassey killed his own mother. And they should not have arrested Mr. Egbor and his son at all. But you know, Oga, I pray for them every day. God will free them. An honest man will not perish for falsehood."

My uncle Papa Ota took Jonathan's matter to Ile-Ife, reputed to be the cradle of Yoruba civilization and seat of an ancient oracular science. It was his own answer to the latest development in the Jonathan Egbor affair—the latest disaster that had overtaken our case. Papa Ota knew someone at Ile-Ife who was reputed to be in direct communication with Oduduwa himself, the founder of the Yoruba dynasty several centuries back. And he was reputed to see far into the future of everybody who, either in person or by proxy, called upon him for a peep into the future. A drastic disease required a drastic cure. While Papa Ota had not lost faith in prayer to the Christian God, he believed that prayer to that Supreme Deity, supplemented by consultation with the diviner at Ife, all went towards achieving the same objective.

Papa Ota came back with information which we already knew—namely, that Jonathan's case was very serious. He also came back with a solution that was a veritable problem. It was a soap preparation which Jonathan and Paul were to use for bathing every day for seven days running. The problem: how were we to smuggle the soap to Jonathan and Paul in the Island Prison? Since the incident in which a VIP suspect attempted suicide in that same prison some nine months before, security had been tightened. The story went that the VIP's wife had bribed the prison authorities to smuggle poison to her husband after an extended family meeting in which it was decided that death was preferable to dishonour through conviction, which was certain in the case. Unfortunately—most unfortunately for all concerned—the doctors had fought round the clock and had succeeded in saving the life of the VIP. After the incident, the Governor had dismissed the Chief Warder and three subordinates for their failure to stop the smuggling of the poison into the prison. Just how were we to smuggle our wonder soap to Jonathan and Paul? In any case, where was the facility for bathing daily in prison custody?

"Do you think that government will kill Jonathan and Paul, Kola?" Papa Ota asked me seriously after we had discussed the difficulty in getting the medicinal soap into the prison.

"I do not think so, Papa Ota," I said. I really did not think that Jonathan and Paul would be hanged for murder, but I must confess that the death of Ojerinde, our star witness for the defence, had considerably shaken my optimism. I was nearly certain now that Bintu Palmer would refuse to come forward to testify for the defence.

"I myself do not think that government will kill him and his son," Papa Ota said. "Baba Ife confirmed that their path is rough. But he saw at the end not death, but life. Does the hand ever come to disaster in its many trips to the mouth during a meal? Jonathan and his son Paul, now in prison, will come back to us alive."

"Amen," I said.

"And we all will be alive when he and his son come back to us."

"Amen," I again said.

I was astounded three days later by a tape which my friend Belo played to me and Bola in my dining-room as we were finishing our evening meal.

"Whose voice is that?" I asked, excitedly.

"Listen again," Belo said as he rewound the tape a little.

After a moment, a voice said, "Someone else who wielded the axe..."

"But that's your voice!" I cried, looking at Belo. He immediately hushed me with a finger on his lips.

The tape continued, but in another voice: "Yes, it was Gilbert Bassey who carried the axe handle which..."

"That's Nwanna's voice!" I cried in ecstasy. "You taped that conversation with him."

"Which conversation is this?" Bola asked, interested.

"Our conversation with Nwanna," I cried. "Where Nwanna confirmed that it was Gilbert Bassey who killed his own mother."

"Very good," she said, seeing the great importance of this to the case.

All three of us now listened to the rest of the tape with as little interruption as possible. It was not perfect, but it was essentially good.

"We've got him, by God!" I cried, towards the end of the tape.

"Yes, and no," Belo said, with much less enthusiasm than either Bola or I showed at the new development.

"But why? What's the matter?" I asked, sensing trouble.

"You see, the Judge may refuse to accept the whole procedure. He may not admit the tape in evidence."

"Is that so?" I asked, disappointed.

"Yes. There are legal reasons why he should not," Belo said.

"Are there no legal reasons why he should?" Bola asked.

"None that I am aware of. Particularly as I was not myself present at the original event to which this tape-recording refers. And the prosecution will most certainly raise serious objection to the tendering of this tape in evidence."

Belo's explanation had now dampened the enthusiasm that the tape had created in me and Bola.

"I will see Oladapo Davies. We will try the tape on the court and see the reaction of both the prosecution and the Judge. In which case I will have to give evidence for the defence. Only way to do it. All will depend on the Judge."

"So much depends on the Judge," Bola sighed.

"Yes, so much depends on the Judge," I echoed after her.

Just why so much depends on these non-infallible humans like me and Belo and my wife Bola, I do not know. I will never know.

TWENTY-ONE

Before the trial resumed again, our case suffered another blow. Bintu Palmer refused to go ahead with her decision to give evidence on our side. While it was something I had suspected immediately after I heard of the death of Ojerinde, I had still hoped and prayed that God might give Sissy Bintu courage to overcome the fear of possible death at the hand of the relatives of the deceased Marian Bassey, who almost everyone now believed were responsible for the death of Ojerinde.

"If I was Bola, your wife, would you say that I should go to give evidence in this case?" Bintu asked me when I pressed her to reconsider her decision.

"Yes, I would," I said without hesitation.

"Would you really?"

"Fact is, Bola would not wait for me to tell her to come forward to give evidence in the circumstances. She would, on her own, decide to do it to save the lives of innocent men."

"She is a brave woman. Very brave woman. But I am not brave."

"Oh no, Sissy Bintu. You are twisting the whole thing now. Who says you are not a brave woman? Of course you are brave. All we are saying..."

"Now I am a twister. First a coward. Now a twister. Thank you."

"Sissy Bintu!" I exclaimed.

"That was just what you said a moment ago. All I want now is to be left alone. I am the only child of my mother. I do not want to die yet."

Belo confirmed that our case had now become so bad that it could not possibly be worse. He decided that we now had no choice but to gamble with our tape-recording of the conversation with Nwanna.

"But do you think the Judge will accept it?" I asked.

"But I've explained that I cannot predict that," he said a little impatiently.

"But man, why don't we tape-record a similar conversation with Sissy Bintu?" I asked excitedly.

"No, good lord, no," Belo laughed. "Our chances of pulling it off with a man are slim. With a woman, they are completely non-existent."

The trial resumed on 15 June '76 with the Government Pathologist giving evidence for the prosecution. He was brief and technical. He confirmed that he had performed the autopsy on the corpse of the late Marian Bassey. She was an African female, well-nourished. There were bruises on the left forearm and the left knee. There was a laceration three centimetres long and half a centimetre deep at the left side of the upper jaw. In his opinion, the deceased had died of a condition which he called by a long Latin name, which was much too difficult for me to remember.

During cross-examination, Dapo Oladapo Davies wanted to know whether or not the deceased could have died from a self-inflicted wound.

No, she could not have inflicted on herself a wound of the type he, the witness, had described.

Could death not have been caused by the deceased falling and knocking her head on the concrete floor?

No, not unless she knocked her head against some object that inflicted the wound. That was, in his opinion, quite unlikely. Could the wound have been caused by a weapon held by someone facing or backing the deceased during a scuffle? Witness did not know.

Was witness certain, beyond any shadow of doubt, that the death of the deceased, Marian Bassey, was due to a premeditated action of the first accused, Jonathan Egbor? No, Witness could not say for certain. Could it be due to any premeditated action on the part of the second accused, Paul Egbor? No. Witness could not say for certain.

Was the pathologist familiar with the effect of an anti-tetanus injection? Yes. Witness was familiar with the effect of an anti-tetanus injection. Was he certain whether or not it could cause death in certain cases? No. Witness could not tell for certain. Was witness certain, beyond any shadow of doubt, that it was not the anti-tetanus injection that was administered to Marian Bassey at the outpatients department at the hospital that killed her? It was most unlikely that the deceased could have been killed by an anti-tetanus injection.

Was he certain of that, beyond reasonable doubt? No, Witness was not.

That closed the case for the prosecution. We were all pleasantly surprised when the Judge announced that if Dapo Oladapo Davies was ready with his first witness, he was ready for the defence opening their case that afternoon. It was already 2 pm, and we had thought that the Judge would call it a day, drawing a neat boundary between the case for the prosecution and the case for the defence. Our lawyer said that he was ready with his first witness, and Alex Belo was put in the witness box after a half-hour adjournment.

I reviewed in my mind the pathetic situation we were in as Belo was being called to the witness box. I remembered that Belo, like all of us, was not present during the fight which led to the unfortunate death of Marian Bassey. So all he would be telling the court would be what he had heard others, who were present at the fight, say. You do not have to be a lawyer to know the near worthlessness of what amounts to hearsay evidence. But Dapo Oladapo Davies said that he would so manage the matter as to get advantage from Belo's evidence and sympathy from the Judge. Belo was a lawyer. No doubt he and Dapo Oladapo Davies knew what they were doing. Who was I, then, to say he was pursuing a wrong line of action? Moreover, does a Yoruba proverb not say that you must look for a missing object even in the most unlikely places? In any case, Belo's evidence would be better than no evidence at all.

The Judge set the whole court roaring with laughter when he wondered whether the learned witness, with a Moslem surname but a Christian first name, would be sworn on the Koran or on the Christian Bible. The witness himself added humorously that he was leading a campaign to add the white candle as an additional object on which witnesses could be sworn, as he was an Aladura, and the Aladura movement was daily making serious inroads into both the Moslem and the Christian preserves. After having been sworn on the Bible, and after having given the usual details of his name, residence, and occupation, the witness confirmed what we all knew: that he neither lived at 22 Fasanya Street nor witnessed the fight which was alleged to have caused the death of Marian Bassey.

"You, in fact, did not know the late Marian Bassey, did you?" Dapo Oladapo Davies asked, adjusting his gown and putting his left leg on the edge of his seat.

"No, I did not."

"Then why have you come forward to give evidence in this case?"

"Because of certain things which I know, and which I am sure will assist the court in this case."

"My Lord," the State Counsel cried, springing to his feet. "This witness has himself admitted that the evidence he is going to give is going to be mere hearsay. He is going to waste the precious time of this honourable court. I respectfully submit to your Lordship that this witness is not competent to give evidence in this case."

The State Counsel sat down smiling at Belo, who himself was smiling in the witness box. These lawyers are so casual in everything they do!

"My Lord, witness is a member of the learned profession and he and I have given careful consideration to the fact that he was not actually a witness to the fight. But, as Your Lordship will soon see, his evidence is going to be of very vital assistance to the court in establishing the truth in this case. And anything that helps the court in that direction, I submit, is evidence that the court should hear."

He too sat down. He too smiled—at his adversary this time.

There followed exchanges between the two lawyers which I must say delighted most of us spectators, even though we did not understand what they were saying. The Judge appeared to be mischievously enjoying the battle between the two. When both lawyers appeared to have exhausted themselves, the Judge asked:

"How many witnesses do you have in all, Mr. Oladapo Davies?"

"Two, m'Lord."

"Only two?"

"Yes, m'Lord."

"In a murder case?" the Judge asked, apparently surprised.

"Yes, m'Lord."

"I must say that this is quite unusual. Most unusual. You will of course be putting the accused persons in the witness box, I presume?"

"Yes, m'Lord."

"In the circumstances, I think I'll allow the evidence of the witness," the Judge announced.

I was very, very happy. So were all our people who again had mustered, in force, in the court.

"As your Lordship pleases," both counsel said the magic formula simultaneously as they both joined the Judge in making notes in their books.

"Mr. Belo, will you now tell the court in your own words what you know about this case?" Mr. Dapo Oladapo Davies said, still scribbling in his book.

"On the evening of Wednesday, 9 June last, my friend Kola Banjo of the housing authority and I called to see a Mr. Philip Nwanna at 22 Fasanya Street, Surulere."

"Was that the house where a fight was alleged to have taken place?"

"Yes."

"How do you come to remember the date, Mr. Belo?"

"I noted it in my diary."

"Please proceed."

"After we had greeted Mr. Nwanna, the three of us started to talk about the alleged fight and the case in court. I asked if Mr. Nwanna was at home on the day of the fight. He confirmed that he was. When I asked him if it was true that it was someone else who wielded the weapon that wounded the woman who died, he said that even though he did not have to speak to me, he would speak because he was not afraid of me because he knew that I was not a CID man. He then said that it was Gilbert Bassey who wielded the weapon that wounded his own mother."

"He, that is Mr. Nwanna, said that it was Gilbert Bassey who wielded the weapon that wounded his own mother," Oladapo Davies repeated slowly.

"Yes, he did," Belo confirmed.

The State Counsel half-rose. Then he sat down without saying anything.

"Gilbert Bassey is the third prosecution witness?" the Judge asked.

"The fourth, m'Lord," Oladapo Davies corrected the Judge respectfully.

"I see."

"And by the mother, Mr. Nwanna was referring to the deceased Marian Bassey?" Oladapo Davies asked.

"That is my understanding," Belo said.

Again the State Counsel rose. And again he sat down without saying anything.

"Please proceed," the Judge said.

"Mr. Nwanna said that Paul Egbor and Gilbert Bassey were fighting and that Jonathan Egbor was trying to separate them."

"Jonathan Egbor is the first accused, and Paul Egbor the second accused, not so?"

"I really don't know them personally. I know them by names only."

"Please proceed."

"Mr. Nwanna said that Gilbert Bassey was ashamed that Paul Egbor had floored him. So after he and Paul Egbor had been separated, he went to bring an axe handle with which he was going to attack Paul Egbor. His mother held on to him and implored him not to use the axe handle as this could lead to the killing of Paul Egbor."

"My Lord," the State Counsel interrupted, "I have great respect for this court. But I am surprised that Your Lordship's magnanimous gesture of goodwill to the defence in their predicament is being abused by my learned friend in this farce they are playing out before the court. My Lord, they are just wasting Your Lordship's precious time."

"But m'Lord..."

"Now, Mr. Macaulay," the Judge cut short our lawyer who was about to reply to the prosecution counsel's criticism.

"Yes, my Lord?"

"I want to say that I understand your concern for both my time and the need to follow proper procedure. I am myself also concerned because the defence has only two witnesses. Two witnesses in a murder case. That, you will agree, is serious."

"Quite, my Lord."

"This is why I've decided to listen to everything the defence has to say. Listen, mark you. I will listen to everything. After listening, I will decide what to accept and what not to accept."

"As your Lordship pleases," the two counsel said in unison. Wasn't I glad at the Judge's decision!

"What happened then, Mr. Belo?" Dapo Oladapo Davies resumed his examination of the witness.

"Mr. Nwanna said that Gilbert Bassey's mother held on to him, trying to wrest the axe handle from him. He accidentally hit the mother on the head."

"He accidentally hit the mother on the head," the lawyer repeated after the witness, writing in his notebook. "What happened then?" the lawyer asked after waiting for the Judge to look up from his writing.

"Then I said: 'So the police are holding the wrong persons?' and Mr. Nwanna said that it was Gilbert Bassey who killed his mother and that everybody in the street knew it and called him a murderer."

"Now who else heard this conversation, Mr. Belo?"

"Mr. Kola Banjo."

"Mr. Kola Banjo," the Judge echoed, his eyes seeking mine where I sat. I was embarrassed. "You are not intending to call him as a witness, I presume?" he asked Oladapo Davies.

"No, m'Lord."

"I'm relieved. I think Mr. Banjo is in this court right now. And I have seen him a number of times here since the case started. Obviously, he cannot be a witness in the circumstances."

"We are not calling Mr. Banjo as a witness, m'Lord."

"I see. No other witness to that conversation, Mr. Oladapo Davies?"

"None, sir."

"None?"

"None, sir."

"What now is the usefulness of Mr. Belo's evidence? He wasn't there during the fight?" the Judge asked, looking at Oladapo Davies.

"No, m'Lord."

"And there's no one else to even corroborate his hearsay evidence."

"No human being, m'Lord."

"Just what are you saying, Mr. Oladapo Davies?" the Judge asked.

"M'Lord, may I proceed with my examination of the witness?"

"Of course, yes. You may proceed."

"Now Mr. Belo, as a lawyer yourself, you see the great defect in your evidence as m'Lord has pointed out. There's great defect in the evidence so far. You see that yourself?"

"Yes. But I took precautions to remove that defect."

"What precautions did you take, Mr. Belo?"

"This..." and here a husky but clearly audible voice issued from the region of the breast pocket of Belo in the witness box: "So he wanted to kill Mr. Egbor? No, he wanted to kill Paul..."

"What's that?" the Judge asked, amazed like everyone else in the court. In addition, he appeared angry.

"A pocket tape-recorder, m'Lord."

"You tape-recorded the conversation?"

"Yes, m'Lord."

"I object seriously to..." the State Counsel was on his feet, angry.

"Wait a minute, wait a minute," the Judge ordered. "Whose voices are those?"

"Partly Mr. Nwanna's. Partly mine, m'Lord."

"Is that the beginning of the tape, Mr. Belo?"

"Not the beginning, m'Lord."

"The end, then?"

"No, m'Lord."

"Is it a long tape?"

"No, m'Lord."

"Will you be seeking to tender this as an exhibit, Mr. Oladapo Davies?"

"Yes, with Your Lordship's permission, I will."

"M'Lord, I object to this contraption being tendered as an exhibit," the State Counsel protested, springing to his feet. "This curious hearsay evidence, producing a tape of an uncorroborated conversation..."

"M'Lord, I do not understand my learned friend's difficulty. Both the witness in the box and the other participant in the conversation that has been taped are defence witnesses. Neither of them is a prosecution witness."

The State Counsel sat down, apparently disarmed. Both counsel now looked to the Judge to indicate the next step, a thing which His Lordship appeared to be in no hurry to do.

Apparently, His Lordship had on his exalted hand a very delicate issue in law. After some time, Mr. Justice Pereira asked:

"Mr. Oladapo Davies, why was it necessary for this witness to tape-record the conversation between himself and another of your own witnesses?"

"Because, m'Lord, the other one is a reluctant witness."

"Will you have to get him here by subpoena?"

"Yes, m'Lord. He's already here, m'Lord."

"You intend taking him today?"

"I would very respectfully plead with Your Lordship that we take him today."

"Today is difficult," His Lordship said, looking at his watch. Mine registered 4.15 pm— give it plus or minus one minute. M'Lord then wrote for a long, long time in his book. I took the opportunity to indulge in a nap. I woke up with a start when the Judge started to speak:

"I fear I cannot see any legal precedent to support the admission of the tape-recording which the defence wishes to tender. I therefore uphold the objection of the prosecution that the tape be not accepted in evidence."

"As Your Lordship pleases," Oladapo Davies said mechanically, showing little concern over a decision that had shattered what might well be our last stand in the battle for the life of Jonathan and that of his son Paul. I groaned inwardly.

"Now, Mr. Oladapo Davies, how much longer do you intend to keep witness in the box?"

"Only one more question, m'Lord."

"With only one more question for Mr. Belo, I may agree to take your other witness today. Otherwise, I'm afraid we may have to adjourn after finishing with Mr. Belo. You may proceed."

"I'm grateful, m'Lord. Now, Mr. Belo, what did Mr. Nwanna tell you made him decide not to come forward to tell the truth?"

"Mr. Nwanna said that he could not come forward to tell the truth in court because he was afraid that if he did, he would be killed."

"Killed! By whom?" the Judge asked, appearing concerned.

"By the relatives of the deceased woman, m'Lord," the witness said.

"I see, I see," the Judge said. "I see."

Here he wrote copiously in his book. After this, he looked up and said: "Proceed."

"That will be all, m'Lord," our lawyer said.

"And you want the next witness now?"

"Immediately, m'Lord."

The Judge then looked at the State Counsel.

"No cross-examination, my Lord," Mr. Macaulay answered the question he read in the Judge's face.

"So you did tape-record the conversation with Nwanna?" Isaiah Erebor asked excitedly when he cornered both Belo and me in the corridor after the court had risen for five minutes.

"Yes, I did," Belo said.

"But, but, but did Mr. Banjo know you were recording the conversation?" he asked, still excited.

"No, he didn't know."

"I didn't know at all," I confirmed.

"Our joint strategy," Dapo Oladapo Davies said. He had joined us in the corridor.

"If Mr. Banjo knew of the recording of the conversation, he might have reacted in a way that—er—"

"Gave the game away?" I concluded the sentence.

"You are right. Your sentimental involvement in the case might have made you overreact to the situation," the lawyer continued. "And if Nwanna knew that we were recording the conversation in his own house, not only would he have switched off, he could have become aggressive."

"You lawyers," I said in wonder and admiration.

"Unfortunately, now it's been of no avail—I mean the tape-recording," Belo said, lighting a cigarette.

"And that's the end of the matter?" I asked.

"You mean the tape-recording? I am afraid yes. The Judge's rejection of it is final," Oladapo Davies said. "Quite final."

Someone beckoned to us from inside that the Judge was about to come in. We all rushed back to the courtroom.

TWENTY-TWO

"Philip Nwanna, you are under oath to speak the truth, the whole truth, and nothing but the truth, with God helping you." Dapo Oladapo Davies reminded the witness in the box after the usual preliminaries. He was our witness—our most reluctant witness. His arrival had been heralded by grave silence and apprehension.

"I will speak the truth," Nwanna promised, hardly beyond a whisper.

"I must ask the witness to speak up," the Judge ordered brusquely. "What did the witness say?"

"Will you repeat what you said, so that this honourable court can hear you properly?" Oladapo Davies asked the witness.

"I said that I will speak the truth," Nwanna said more audibly.

"You said that you will speak the truth," Oladapo Davies repeated, writing. "Yes."

"But it is not enough to speak the truth, Mr. Nwanna. You are under oath to speak the whole truth. And you will speak nothing, nothing whatsoever—but the truth. Now tell this honourable court what you know of the fight at

22 Fasanya Street on 28 January 1975. You have already told the court that you live at that address."

"I know that two people were fighting that day."

"Which two people were fighting that day?"

"The two people fighting were Paul Egbor and Gilbert Bassey."

"The two people fighting were Paul Egbor and Gilbert Bassey. Do you now see any of them in this court?"

"Yes, that one there," the witness said, pointing in the direction of the two men in the dock.

"Which one is that? Paul Egbor or Gilbert Bassey?"

"Paul Egbor." Nwanna now began to speak up.

"Paul Egbor. That is the second accused, m'Lord," Oladapo Davies said, stating what the Judge and everyone else in the court already knew. Then the two counsel and the Judge all wrote copiously in their books.

Now you have seen Paul Egbor in the court. Have you seen the other participant in the fight here in the court?"

The witness in the box scanned all the faces in the court. I felt quite uneasy as our eyes met. I felt I had betrayed Nwanna. I don't know how

Belo had felt when his and Nwanna's eyes met, as I know they must have done. But then Belo was a lawyer. And lawyers have no feeling.

"Yes, I have seen Gilbert Bassey in the court," the witness said.

"Where is he?"

"Over there," the witness indicated the direction where Gilbert Bassey sat.

I was pleasantly surprised that he had not effected his escape before this moment. Presumably, that would have drawn greater attention to him when walking out than when he sat down.

"Tell the court what you saw happen when the two men were fighting."

"I came out to see what was happening when I heard the noise in the compound."

"You came out of where, Mr. Nwanna?"

"I came out of my room."

"You came out of your room. Then what did you see after you came out of your room?"

"I saw Paul Egbor and Gilbert Bassey fighting."

"Then what happened after that, Mr. Nwanna?"

"I saw Mr. Jonathan Egbor and some other people separating them."

"What happened after that?"

"When they had been separated, I went back into my room."

"Then what happened after that? Tell the court what happened. You are doing quite well so far."

"But Mr. Oladapo Davies..."

"Yes, m'Lord?"

"Why won't you allow the court to decide which witness is doing well and which is not?"

"I was reading Your Lordship's transparent mind, m'Lord!"

They all laughed, but we dared not laugh.

"What happened after that?" Mr. Nwanna repeated the question.

"Yes. What happened after that?"

"I heard more shouting in the compound. But I did not come out of my room."

"What kind of shouting did you hear in the compound?"

"I heard people shouting. I thought perhaps Paul Egbor and Gilbert Bassey were fighting again."

"You, in fact, knew that Paul Egbor and Gilbert Bassey were fighting again. Why did you not come out of your room to assist in separating them?"

"Because the two boys are too fond of fighting. Many people in our compound are tired of their fighting."

"But all the same, other people came out to help in separating them. Why did you not come out?"

"I was tired of seeing them fight. I was tired and I was not feeling well."

"What happened after you heard people shouting?"

"I heard that Mrs. Bassey had been wounded."

"You did not see her wounded yourself?"

"No. I was in my room."

"Whose voice did you hear say that Mrs. Bassey had been wounded?"

"I don't know. Many people were shouting at the same time."

"Then what happened?"

"When there was no more noise in the compound, I came out of my room."

"Who did you see then?"

"I saw two girls. They said Mrs. Bassey was wounded and that she had gone to the hospital."

"Now, Mr. Nwanna, I remind you again that you are under oath to speak not just the truth, but the whole truth. And what is equally important, nothing but the truth."

"Yes, I am speaking the truth," Nwanna said, hardly above a whisper.

"But only part of the truth, not the whole truth, Mr. Nwanna. And what little truth that you are speaking is being coated with plenty of untruth. You will have to try again."

"I am speaking the truth."

"Are you speaking the whole truth?" the Judge demanded. "Counsel wants to know if you are speaking the whole truth. And I tell you something as a friend. He is a clever lawyer. So you had better speak the truth and speak the whole truth. And don't try any lies on him. He has a lie detector in his pocket. Proceed, Mr. Oladapo Davies," the Judge said after the laughter had subsided.

"I am grateful, m'Lord. Now, Mr. Nwanna, you know Mr. Kola Banjo?"

"Mr. Kola Banjo?" Nwanna asked, instinctively looking in my direction. But merciful heavens—his eyes failed to register contact with mine.

"Yes, Kola Banjo. Do you know him?"

"Yes, I know him."

"Have you seen him in court today?"

"Yes," Nwanna said uneasily.

"Do you remember certain conversations you had with Mr. Banjo?"

"I have had many conversations with Mr. Banjo before. I don't know which one you mean," Nwanna said, getting visibly more uneasy.

"You know which conversation I mean alright. We will come back to that presently. But tell the court now, do you know Mr. Belo?"

"Mr. Belo?" the witness looked genuinely puzzled.

"Yes, Alex Belo."

"Mr. Alex Belo? I don't remember."

"Do you not remember a conversation on the evening of 9 June between you, Mr. Banjo, and Mr. Belo in your parlour in which you told the two men something about the fight?"

The witness stared at the defense lawyer. He slowly looked round the court till his eyes rested on mine momentarily. But only momentarily, as I immediately lowered my eyes in embarrassment and near shame. But I knew I did what I did in the interest of truth, which truth would free Jonathan and Paul.

"Mr. Nwanna, do you remember the things you told Mr. Banjo of the Lagos Housing Authority and Mr. Belo of the Nigerian Ports Authority? Do you remember, or do you not remember, the things you told them about the fight that took place in your compound on 28 January 1975?"

"No," Nwanna muttered.

"Do you remember that you told the two men that you saw the whole fight?"

"No," the witness again muttered.

"And that you, in fact, told them that you saw Gilbert Bassey wield the weapon that wounded his mother?"

"No!" Nwanna shouted from the dock, as if he had just received a new set of energy-supplying batteries.

"And that you would not come to court to say what you were then telling them because you were afraid?"

"No."

"You deny these things, I see," the defense counsel said slowly. "And now, Mr. Nwanna, did you know one Emmanuel Ojerinde?" he asked, on a change of subject.

"Emmanuel Ojerinde?"

"Yes. Emmanuel Ojerinde."

"Yes, I knew him."

"In what connection did you know him?"

"He was my co-tenant."

"He was your co-tenant at 22 Fasanya Street, not so?"

"Yes."

"He doesn't live at 22 Fasanya Street anymore, does he?"

No reply.

"Where does Emmanuel Ojerinde live now?" Oladapo Davies thundered.

"I don't know."

"You know, my friend. Where does Emmanuel Ojerinde, who once lived at 22 Fasanya Street, live now?"

"He has died."

"Yes, he's dead. You, in fact, know that he is dead. M'Lord, Emmanuel Ojerinde was to be our chief witness. He was lined up to give evidence. He expressed anxiety that he might be killed if he gave evidence. He died in a motorcycle accident twelve days ago. That was before he had a chance of giving evidence."

Wheeling round to face the witness box, the lawyer cleared his throat and said in measured terms:

"I put it to you, Philip Nwanna, that you in fact saw Gilbert Bassey wield the weapon that felled his own mother, the deceased Marian Bassey." He fixed the unhappy man in the witness box.

"No," Nwanna muttered.

"I put it to you that you have lied to this court that you did not see Gilbert Bassey wield the axe handle that felled his mother because you are afraid of harassment by the police."

"No, I am not afraid of the police."

"And I put it to you that you have lied also because you think that if you tell the truth about how Marian Bassey died, the juju of the relatives of Marian Bassey would kill you, as you and people like you now believe that it was this same juju that killed Emmanuel Ojerinde."

"No. I am not afraid," Nwanna said, visibly frightened.

"That will be all for this witness, m'Lord," Barrister Oladapo Davies said with a note of dejection in his voice. He sat down, mopping his brow with a silk handkerchief.

The Judge wrote endlessly in his book after our lawyer had sat down. So did the State Counsel and our lawyer's junior. They wrote for a long, long time. I admired Oladapo's eloquence. He was truly brilliant. I again wished that I too was a lawyer.

But what was the net effect of Oladapo Davies's brilliant examination of Nwanna? Nothing, as far as one could see. Nwanna had told all the lies and had got away with it. The tape recording—Belo's ingenious device for catching the coward and liar—had been refused in evidence by the Judge. Nearly everybody else but the Judge knew that the bastard was telling lies. Yet he had refused to admit in evidence the one thing that would show him what he did not know, but what everyone else knew. Yet he refused even to let the tape be played in court.

What kind of legal system was this that had a built-in mechanism for not allowing the truth to come out? What kind of legal system was this that saw a witness telling such awful lies on the so-called oath and yet wrote down such evidence in the records of the court? Was our Jonathan going to be killed because of the illogicality in this terrible legal system?

"Any cross-examination, Mr. Macaulay?" The Judge's question brought me back from my daydreaming. All the time, he had been writing copiously in his book.

"None, my Lord," the State Counsel announced, with a shrug of his shoulders.

TWENTY-THREE

Our case suffered yet another serious setback. A day after the last sitting at which we drew a blank with Philip Nwanna, Mr. Justice Labo Pereira was taken to hospital for an undisclosed illness. After nine days in bed at the General Hospital in Lagos, he was flown out of the country for specialist treatment in Britain. I understand that the conditions of service of judges and of a number of very senior public servants included provision for such medical treatment overseas at public expense!

I was really not interested in how much the medical treatment of m'Lord Justice Labo Pereira cost the Nigerian taxpayer. After all, that was a case of the heavens crashing onto the earth. That would not be a disaster for individual concern, but the concern of all the thousands of millions of people inhabiting this planet. After all, why should I worry about the paltry twenty or thirty kobo of my own tax that would go into the pocket of an overpaid, overfed Harley Street specialist through his medical treatment of a Nigerian judge?

Why could the case of State versus Jonathan Egbor and Paul Egbor not be continued by another judge while Pereira was away ill in

London? That was what we wanted to know, all of us interested in the case. My friend Belo's explanation was that the judge who started such a case must continue it. What an explanation! What happens if he dies, or becomes completely incapacitated, half living, half dead? What happens then? Belo's answer: another judge would start the case all over again!

We prayed from the bottom of our heart that Mr. Justice Labo Pereira should get well quickly. But the illness of undisclosed nature ran its course. We ran from pillar to post. But we got that same answer: No one except Mr. Justice Pereira was competent to continue the case. We just had to wait until he came back from London.

In between, Raliatu disappeared into her husband's hometown in the Benin hinterland. I heard later that her people back home had arranged an appointment for her to see a big Mallam. He was supposed to do things for her that would make whatever her husband and her son said at that crucial stage of the case—when they were due to give evidence—be wholly pleasing and acceptable to the high and mighty Mr. Justice Pereira.

Raliatu came back three days before the Judge himself arrived back from Britain on Friday, 17 September. We thought that he would start sitting the very following Monday. No, he did not. In fact, the case did not reopen until thirteen days after his arrival back from Britain.

And that was three whole months and fifteen days after the last sitting. It was three months and fifteen days of continued suffering for Jonathan Egbor and his son Paul Egbor in prison custody. Needless, preventable suffering, all because one judge was ill out of a total of twenty-one in the State Judiciary!

After the Judge had taken his seat, all counsel present rose one by one to say words of congratulations and wishes of complete recovery to the judge. After he had thanked them all for their expressions of goodwill, Dapo Oladapo Davies put Jonathan Egbor in the witness box.

Poor Jonathan! The suffering in prison custody and the anxiety caused by the three months and fifteen days of inactivity occasioned by the Judge's illness now showed clearly on his face. Why, oh why, in the name of God, should the innocent suffer this much, this long?

The clerk took him through the ritual of swearing, and Dapo Oladapo Davies asked him the details of his full name, where he lived, and what work he did.

"You know why you are here in this court, Mr. Egbor?"

"Yes," Jonathan muttered.

"Why are you here?"

"They said that we killed Mrs. Bassey."

"Which people said that you killed Mrs. Bassey?"

"The police. And Mr. Bassey. And Gilbert Bassey. They all are telling lies against me and Paul."

"Now Mr. Egbor, I want you to tell the court exactly what happened on the day there was a fight at 22 Fasanya Street. And I want you to tell truthfully how the whole thing happened."

"In the morning I went to work. Even at work I did not feel well. I wanted to go to the hospital because I did not feel well."

"Mr. Egbor, I want you to limit your evidence to what you saw and what you did during the fight at 22 Fasanya Street. Did you take part in the fight at 22 Fasanya Street?"

"Not at all!" Jonathan said most expressively in the witness box. "I never fight before."

"You never fought before. Did you fight that day?"

"Not at all."

"Who fought then?"

"It was Gilbert Bassey who fought Paul."

"That is the fourth prosecution witness and the second accused, m'Lord."

"The fourth prosecution witness and the second accused were fighting," the Judge repeated, writing it in his book.

"Proceed, Mr. Egbor," the lawyer said.

"Even I was in my room when I heard people shouting in the corridor."

"When you heard people shouting in the corridor, what did you do?"

"I came out of my room. Even though I was tired, and I was not well, still I came out."

"Why did you come out?"

"I must come out because I heard the voice of Paul shouting in the corridor."

"What did you see when you came out into the corridor?"

"I saw Gilbert fighting with Paul."

"Go on. What else did you see?"

"I saw people trying to separate them."

"What did you do then?"

"I started to separate them. But the two boys were stubborn. They did not want to be separated. Then I told Paul in Esala language that if he was truly my son and not a bastard, he should stop fighting."

"And did he stop fighting then?"

"Yes. He stopped fighting."

"So he is your son, and not a bastard?"

"Yes, he is my son. Don't you see his face, that he resembles me very much?"

Both the defence counsel's question and Jonathan Egbor's answer raised laughter.

"After you had separated them, after the second accused had stopped fighting, what happened?"

"Paul—that is my son—went out into the street. And I went back into my room to sleep because I did not feel well. Even I wanted to go to the chemist. But I was still tired."

"What happened after that?" Dapo Oladapo Davies asked somewhat impatiently.

"I heard shouting in the corridor again. I came out and saw that they were fighting again."

"But you said that Paul Egbor—that is the second accused—had gone out. How come then that he was fighting in the corridor again?"

"You see my trouble now," Jonathan Egbor declared bitterly. "As soon as I went to my room, the foolish boy came back to the house. And as soon as Gilbert Bassey saw him, they started fighting again. If that foolish boy had not come back, how could I have been in this trouble? It is now nearly two years that I have been in this trouble. And now..."

"Mr. Egbor, you must limit your answers to the question," Dapo Oladapo Davies warned him. "Everyone is sorry about your plight. But when you make your answers to questions short, then we will make quick progress. And the case will soon be over. You saw them fighting in the corridor again when you came out of your room?"

"Yes, they were fighting again. And people were separating them again. And I too began to separate them."

"Who were the other people separating them?"

"Even many people were separating them."

"Name some of them."

"Mrs. Akpan was one of them."

"Yes? Who else was separating them?"

"You want me to name more people?"

"Yes, name more. That's what I want you to do."

"Mrs. Bassey. She too was separating them."

"Mrs. Bassey. That is the deceased woman?"

"Yes."

"Any more?"

"Even plenty of people were separating them."

"Who are the others?"

"I don't even remember now. You don't know how it is, after nearly two years since that the fight took place, and I have been put in this trouble?"

"Mr. Egbor, you must try and remember who the other people were that were trying to separate Gilbert Bassey and Paul Egbor when they were fighting. Was Mr. Bassey one of them? I mean Gilbert's father, the first prosecution witness. Was he there separating the two boys who were fighting?"

"No. Don't you know that he had not come back from work at the time they were fighting?"

"I do not know because I was not there. You were there. And you should not answer my questions with questions. What you have said now I take to mean that Mr. Bassey Etim Bassey was not one of the people separating the two men fighting?"

"Mr. Bassey was not there."

"Which man was there? You have given us the names of two women."

"Which man was there? I say I don't remember," he shrugged his shoulders dejectedly.

At this stage, all of us in the court had become worried about Jonathan's inability to name one or two of the men. In particular, why had he not mentioned Nwanna? Could it be true that twenty months in custody had destroyed his memory completely?

"You know Mr. Nwanna, Mr. Egbor?" the lawyer asked a leading question.

"Yes. Even Mr. Nwanna was one of the people trying to separate them at first."

The State Counsel at first rose to his feet, apparently to protest against the leading question. But he immediately sat down again, apparently coming to the conclusion that it wasn't worthwhile doing this.

"Did you yourself join in separating them?"

"Yes."

"And the deceased woman—was she separating them too?"

"At first she too was separating them. But later she joined her son in beating Paul and me. You see, Paul had floored the son, and we were trying to drag Paul away from the top of her son."

"That son is Gilbert Bassey, second prosecution witness, m'Lord," Dapo Oladapo Davies explained for the benefit of his Lordship.

"Thank you, counsel," the Judge said.

"Did you say the woman was beating even you, when you were not fighting with her? Or were you fighting with her?"

"Not at all. Everyone saw her beating me. She even gave me a human bite on the back."

"She gave you a human bite on the back?" the Judge exclaimed. "Really?"

"God is my witness. I never lie," Jonathan said, immediately proceeding to unbutton his shirt—a preliminary operation calculated to lead to exposing the seat of the human bite.

"And did you bite her back?" the Judge asked.

"Not at all. I never bite human being before," he declared seriously.

"Not a good thing to do, I assure you. In any case, what do you bite, Mr. Egbor?" the Judge asked humorously.

"Meat. And panla," Jonathan said, laughing in spite of his misery.

"Panla is dried stockfish, m'Lord," Dapo Oladapo Davies explained.

"What did you do when the woman was beating and biting you?"

"I raised up my two hands."

"Why?"

"Don't you know she is a married woman?" Jonathan Egbor asked seriously.

"I know she was. All the same, why did you raise your two hands?"

"Because she is a married woman. It is our custom in my town that a man must not touch a married woman that is not his wife. I raised up my hands and everyone saw that I did not touch her."

"What happened after this?"

"When Paul was dragged from the top of Gilbert, I told him that if he was my son and not a bastard, he must go out of the house."

"And did he go out of the house?"

"Yes."

"And what happened after that?"

"I went to my room. You know I was not well."

"You have said so. What happened after?"

"Then I heard people shouting again. When I came out, I saw Gilbert holding an axe handle. And people were running away from him."

"Go on."

"When he saw me, he wanted to hit me with the axe handle."

"What did you do then?"

"I ran away from him."

"You ran away from him. Why did you run away from him, Mr. Egbor?"

"Why? Don't you know that if I did not run away, he would kill me?"

"Alright, what happened after that?"

"He ran towards Paul. He wanted to kill him."

"He ran towards Paul. He..."

"But wait a minute, wait a minute," the Judge interrupted Dapo Oladapo Davies. "The last note I have made about Paul Egbor was that the witness told him that if he was his son and not a bastard, he should go away from the house."

"Yes, m'Lord," Dapo Oladapo Davies confirmed.

"And Paul Egbor, not being a bastard, went away from the house."

"Yes, m'Lord."

"But here we now have this same Paul Egbor being chased with an axe handle by Gilbert Bassey in the house. Has he now become a bastard?" The Judge's question raised laughter.

"But the foolish boy had come back again," Jonathan wailed from the witness box.

"Paul Egbor had come back again," the lawyer said. "And you said you saw Gilbert run towards him with an axe handle. Was that what you said?"

"Yes, sir. He ran towards him with the axe handle. His mother was holding him back begging him not to kill Paul."

"His mother was begging him not to kill Paul. What happened after?" the lawyer asked.

"He accidentally hit his mother on the head!"

"You said he accidentally hit his mother on the head. Was that with the axe handle?"

"Yes, it was with the axe handle."

"How do you know it was accidental?"

"But which person will hit his own mother with an axe handle, if not by mistake? It must be accidental."

"What happened after that?"

"What happened after that? Mrs. Bassey fell down. And when she fell down she was crying."

"What was she saying when she was crying?"

"She was saying: 'Gilbert has killed me, Gilbert has killed me'."

"Did other people in the corridor hear her say this?"

"Yes."

"Witness must limit himself to what he heard, certainly not what others heard," the Judge rebuked the witness and, by implication, the lawyer. "How can he know what others heard or did not hear?"

"Did anyone else say or do anything after this?"

"Mrs. Akpan. She cried like this: 'Gilbert done kill 'im mother'. And everyone heard her say so."

"That is the second prosecution witness. But you heard her say in this court that she did not see anything and that she did not hear anything?"

"Don't you see that she was lying? Don't you remember that she herself confessed that she was afraid of the Judge? Even I wanted to challenge her, but I too was afraid of the Judge."

"But you challenged Gilbert Bassey, didn't you?" the lawyer asked him.

"But don't you see that the lies of that one were too many? He told too many lies, and that was the reason why I challenged him. But even when I challenged him, did you and the Judge not shout at me to keep quiet?"

"You see, Mr. Egbor, this is a High Court. It is not the Mushin Customary Court where many people speak at the same time," the lawyer explained. "Here in the High Court only the witness—one witness—can speak at one time. And he must speak from the witness box, where you are now. Only counsel like me or the State Counsel and the Judge can ask him questions. And he must give his answers without anyone interrupting him. And..."

"But when a witness is lying against an accused person, can the accused person not cry out that he is lying?" Jonathan asked seriously.

"No, he cannot. The accused person will have his own turn to come into the witness box to give his own version of what happened. He then has a chance of proving that a particular witness has been lying. You see what I mean?"

Jonathan shook his head sadly. He certainly did not see the wisdom in what the lawyer had been saying. He did not see the sense in a legal system in which a witness who tells a lie is allowed to go unchallenged immediately, while the lie is still hot.

"And Mr. Egbor," the counsel said, "there is one other thing you must know. When you are there in the witness box, you must only answer questions put to you by counsel. You must not ask questions. You understand?"

Jonathan again shook his head sadly. He did not see the reason why he should not ask questions for the clarification of issues he did not understand.

"Counsel may proceed," the Judge ordered.

"You heard the evidence of Mr. Nwanna, Mr. Egbor? That's the second defence witness, m'Lord."

Jonathan looked at his lawyer apprehensively.

"Did you hear the evidence of the second defence witness?"

"Yes. I heard him. I heard the lies he told that..."

"Listen Mr. Egbor. You must not race ahead of me," Dapo Oladapo Davies said impatiently. "Did you hear the evidence? Yes or No. That is all I want at this stage. Now, did you hear the evidence?"

"I heard the lies he told. And..."

"Mr. Egbor, you must..."

"I think counsel should allow witness to continue the way he knows," the Judge ordered. "Even though it is an unorthodox method of giving evidence, let him continue."

"As Your Lordship pleases. Now Mr. Egbor, you heard the evidence of Mr. Nwanna?"

"Yes, I heard the lies he told. And I asked myself why he was telling lies against me when he knew that myself and my son can be killed by the government for a murder which we never committed. Yet he was my friend, and he was telling this dangerous lie. Then I know he was afraid of the police. And he was afraid that other people would kill him for giving true evidence. They all know the truth. They all saw that bad boy Gilbert when he took the handle and hit his mother with it. But they are all afraid to speak the truth. They now want me and my son to die for murder."

Here Jonathan broke down.

"Now Mr. Egbor, when the deceased woman fell down, what did you do?" the lawyer asked after Jonathan had recovered sufficiently to continue.

"I was afraid when she cried that Gilbert had killed her."

"Had Gilbert actually killed her?" the Judge asked.

"Gilbert had wounded her," Jonathan said.

"Yes. Someone had only wounded her. If she had been killed she would not be capable of speaking, would she? Now proceed."

"So I ran to the police station."

"Which police station?" the lawyer asked.

"Mainland Police Station No. 2."

"What happened there?"

"I told the officer there that there was a serious fight at 22 Fasanya Street."

"What did he tell you?"

"He told me to go to the hospital to get treatment for my human bite first."

"Did you tell him of the human bite?" the lawyer asked.

"Yes, I showed it to him. Then he told me to go and get treatment at the hospital, and to come back to make a statement at the police station the following day."

"Did you go to get treatment in the hospital?"

"Even I waited in the outpatients' place for many hours."

"Did you get treatment eventually?"

"Yes."

"And did you go to the police station the following day?"

"Yes. I went to the police station."

"What time was that?"

"About 10 in the morning."

"What happened then?"

"The officer I saw asked for my name. When I told him, he went inside for a long time. When he came back, another officer followed him."

"Then what happened?"

"The other officer that followed the first officer asked for my name. When I told him, he asked if I lived at 22 Fasanya Street. When I told him that I lived at 22 Fasanya Street, he asked me to follow him inside the station."

"Did you follow him?"

"Yes."

"Where did he take you?"

"Inside the station. When we reached the cell, he opened it and asked me to go inside."

"He asked you to get inside the cell?"

"Yes. And I asked him why I should get inside the cell. Was it not a statement I came to make at the police station? Why should I get inside the cell for that? I then saw why many people are afraid to go to the police station. If a man comes to the police station to make a statement, why should the police put him in cell?"

"I too don't know, Mr. Egbor," the lawyer said. "But what did you do then?"

"He said: 'Don't you know the woman you fought has died?'"

"He told you that the woman you fought had died. And were you surprised?"

"I was very surprised. At first I could not believe him. I asked: 'Which woman?' He said:

'Mrs. Bassey.' And I asked: 'Is she dead?' And he said: 'Yes'."

"And what did you say then?"

"I said: 'May her soul rest in peace'," and here Jonathan made the sign of the cross in the witness box, to the amusement of everyone in the court, the Judge himself leading the laughter.

"And did you eventually make a statement to the police?"

"I made even two. Not only one. They made me make statement two times. Once I made a statement at Mainland Police Station No. 2. I made a second statement at Central CID."

"Were you taken from Mainland Police Station No. 2 to Central CID on the Island?"

"After I had suffered for three weeks or nineteen days, they transferred me and Paul to Central CID. There I made a second statement."

"Did you write the statement yourself, Mr. Egbor?"

"No. The CID man wrote it as I talked to him."

"Did he read it to you after he finished writing?"

"Yes, he read it to me."

"Did he write it correctly, as you told him?"

"Yes."

"And is this the statement?" Dapo Oladapo Davies asked the clerk for the document. This was shown to Jonathan in the witness box. "Can you read English?"

"I can read a little."

"You can read that statement?"

"Small."

"Never mind, I will read it presently. Meanwhile you see the signature at the bottom of the statement. Is that your signature?"

"Yes."

The lawyer at this stage sought leave of the court to tender the document as an exhibit. It was duly registered. He then read out the statement, reading twice by way of emphasis the portion where Jonathan had said that the deceased woman had cried that Gilbert had killed her, and the portion where Elizabeth Akpan had said that Gilbert had killed his own mother.

"Do you agree that that was the statement you made to the police?"

"That was the second statement, the one I made at the CID. I first made one at the Mainland Police Station No. 2. That one is not here."

"Yes. Is that one different from this one?"

"No. It is the same thing. I never say one thing today and say another thing tomorrow. I never lie," Jonathan declared.

"Good. Very good. That will be all, m'Lord," the lawyer said, wiping the beads of perspiration from his face with a clean handkerchief.

"Good. Very good," the Judge repeated the words of Dapo Oladapo Davies after he had finished recording the last piece of the examination in chief in his book. "Any cross-examination, Mr. Macaulay?"

"No, my Lord," the State Counsel said, to the surprise and relief of all of us.

"No cross-examination at all?" the Judge asked again.

"No, my Lord," again the State Counsel confirmed.

"In which case witness may step down," the Judge ordered.

TWENTY-FOUR

Paul Egbor gave his evidence for the defence the following day. I thought that he performed quite well both in his evidence in chief and in the cross-examination by Macaulay, the State Counsel. His evidence substantially followed the same lines as Jonathan's. He demonstrated how Gilbert Bassey had gone into his father's room, how he had come out with an axe handle, and how his mother had been hit on the face with the axe handle when Gilbert swung it back to collect momentum for a forward stroke meant for him, Paul. He corroborated the evidence of his father, Jonathan, that the stricken woman had moaned in pain on the floor, saying that Gilbert had killed her. He also confirmed that Elizabeth Akpan had screamed at the sight of the fallen woman that Gilbert had killed his own mother.

Both counsel also addressed the court that day. The State Counsel marshalled legal arguments why the Judge should believe the prosecution's story that the late Marian Bassey had, in fact, died as a result of a fight in which both Jonathan Egbor and his son Paul had struck down the unfortunate woman. For this reason, he insisted, they must both be found guilty of murder. As usual, he cited a number of legal authorities to support his case. On the other

331

hand, our lawyer Dapo Oladapo Davies argued most brilliantly that the prosecution had failed woefully to show that the ingredients of murder had been established in the case. He too cited several legal authorities to show that, even if the court believed that a murder had been committed, the prosecution had failed to prove beyond all reasonable doubt that the murder had in fact been committed by the two accused persons. Were we all not impressed by his eloquence? I wondered how, like Oliver Goldsmith's village schoolmaster, such a small head carried so much law and learning.

The Judge then reserved judgement for 22 October. That was three long weeks away—another twenty-one days of suffering for Jonathan and Paul in police custody. But then, what was twenty-one days compared with the near twenty-one months since the trouble started? We all immediately began to look forward to the day when we prayed our dear Jonathan and his son Paul would be set free.

Bola and I were still in bed the morning after the last sitting when we heard Raliatu's sobbing downstairs. We exchanged ominous glances. We were in trouble again. We wondered what it was this time. She slipped on her housecoat and hurried downstairs. She came back moments later with the newspapers.

"There's been trouble in the prison, Daddy," she said, exhibiting the front page of the Times.

"BLACK MARIA HORROR," the headline screamed. I jumped out of bed and snatched the paper from her. I raced through the news under the headline.

There was pandemonium yesterday outside the gate of the Island Prison in Lagos as horror-stricken warders and policemen took to their heels on discovering that more than half the suspects brought back from the various courts had died in the Black Maria that was carrying them. The discovery was made by a warder when he opened the door of the vehicle and ordered the suspected persons to come out. Instead of their coming out, a number of dead bodies fell out of the door, while a number of others lay huddled together on the floor of the vehicle.

Only a handful of men staggered out of the Black Maria. These all collapsed as soon as they had taken a few wobbling steps outside. A few moans indicated that there were still a handful of men not yet completely dead among the bodies that were lying in a heap on the floor of the vehicle. A bold warder clambered up the vehicle to isolate the dead from the living and to bring out the latter one by one for first aid treatment.

Both police and warders had difficulty in keeping back the crowd of onlookers that immediately gathered outside the prison gate. Many of these cried in sympathy with the wives and children of the many men, though unknown, who were lying dead both in the vehicle and on the grass. "What now will happen to their families?" an elderly woman sobbed, holding her breasts.

When our correspondent approached the senior warder for details of what actually happened, he was told by the official that he was not allowed to speak to newspapermen. When our News Editor rang the Public Relations Officer of the Prison Department for information, a female voice said that he was away on emergency duty in the Island Prison.

The headline in the Monitor read "SHOCK DEATHS IN BLACK MARIA." It said that forty-three out of the sixty-eight suspected persons in the Black Maria had died and that nineteen others had been rushed to the General Hospital, where they lay between life and death as doctors fought desperately to save their lives.

The BBC carried the news in its "News of the African World" bulletin at 6:15 am. It said that reports reaching London from Lagos said that a number of suspected persons being transported from various Lagos courts back to custody at the main city prison had died of suffocation in the Black Maria carrying them.

I raced through my ablutions and short-circuited breakfast. How could I eat in the face of such news? I must be on the road immediately to beat the 8 o'clock traffic congestion into the Island. I left Bola to manage Raliatu as best as she could. I must find out immediately what had happened to Jonathan and Paul.

Police diverted traffic away from the vicinity of the Island Prison, and I had to park some distance away. I then joined the large crowd of people who jammed the three access roads to the prison. Some hundred metres away from the gate, it became practically impossible to move due to the density of the crowd. I saw, from afar, the police baton-charging the crowd at intervals to prevent them from physically breaking into the gaol house. I was disappointed that I couldn't get any nearer and that I wasn't going to get any information about Jonathan and Paul.

"Do you think it is true that many people in custody have died?" I asked a man who I thought could have some information.

"What a question," the man retorted. "Didn't you see the two ambulances that drove past half an hour ago?"

"No, I have just come," I told him.

"Many, many people died in the Black Maria. And many, many more people died in the riots in the prison," the man said.

"Are there riots in the prison then?" I asked.

"Two warders and six prisoners have been killed," the man said, trying to steady himself against the push from the front.

"Master, it is not two warders," another man said, "it is five. I saw five warders and eleven prisoners dead with my own eyes. But government will tell lies when they give out the official announcement tomorrow. You watch. They will say only one warder was killed and—eh, stop pushing me, can't you see?" the man cried in protest against another man who was himself trying desperately to keep his balance in the crowd.

It was no use. It was impossible to get to the front. That meant I wasn't going to get any information about Jonathan and Paul. I must now extricate myself from the crowd and go to the hospital. I would check from the wounded persons admitted to beds in the wards and from the bodies in the public mortuary. I eventually succeeded in getting away from the crowd and made for the car. In a short time, I was at the hospital. I made for the office of a doctor friend.

He confirmed seventeen casualties of the Black Maria were in bed in Ward G. He volunteered to take me there. The crowd of curious onlookers and relatives in the corridors made way for the doctor in a white coat, and in no time we were in the emergency ward.

"Good morning, sir," someone greeted me as we entered the ward.

"Mr. Erebor," I said in recognition. "Is Jonathan alright?" I asked breathlessly.

"Yes, sir. He's in bed 19."

"You mean Jonathan is in this ward?" I asked, relieved that he was here in the ward and not in the mortuary.

"Yes, sir," he confirmed, as he led both the doctor and me towards bed 19.

"Are you alright, Jonathan?" I asked quietly, taking the cue from the doctor who tiptoed the last few steps to the bed.

The figure in the bed did not say a thing. His head was heavily bandaged, with his eyes, nose, and mouth defined by mere slits in the bandage. His right arm was in a white cast. There was a drip on his left arm.

"Jonathan, are you alright?" I again asked, laying my hand on his left shoulder. The doctor was checking the charts on the white card at the bedstead. His bed was inclined the wrong way.

"Jonathan, can you hear me?" I asked anxiously. "Are you alright?"

He nodded his head. But he said nothing.

"Is he alright?" I turned to the doctor.

"He will be alright," he said. "He hasn't completely recovered yet. He isn't really aware of your presence or who you are."

"But he's going to be alright?"

"Of course he's going to be alright. I think we had better leave him now."

Jonathan I had seen—alive, but just alive. But what about Paul? I asked Erebor as we were coming out of the ward.

"Paul is alright, sir."

"Is he here in the hospital too?"

"No, sir. He's in the prison yard."

"He wasn't injured in the Black Maria?" I asked.

"No, sir. He's alright, sir."

Paul was alright. My friend Police Superintendent Dada confirmed this from the Chief Warder later in the day. I was allowed to see him the following evening. In spite of the nuisance I knew she could be, I brought Raliatu with me. I also brought Bola. And as was now usual, the Chief Warder offered me the comfort of his own room.

Raliatu embraced Paul as he was led into the room by a warder. "Paul, Paul, thank God," she muttered again and again, sinking to her knees and rolling on the floor in an act of profound gratitude to God who had delivered her son from the jaws of death.

"Good evening, sir; good evening, ma," the boy greeted both Bola and myself.

"You are alright, Paul?" I asked him. He looked alright. There was still a little crowd of onlookers outside and they made a lot of noise. So one had to shout to be heard.

"I'm O.K., sir."

"Were you in the Black Maria too, Paul?" I asked him.

"I was in the Black Maria, sir. We were all in the Black Maria."

"What happened?" I asked. The Chief Warder had gone out of the room to arrange for more warders to join those keeping the crowd back outside.

"We were too many, sir, and people were fighting."

"Why were they fighting, Paul?"

"People wanted to get to the windows at the side of the Black Maria. Everybody wanted to get fresh air from the windows because it was too hot. And those who were already at the windows did not want to leave there for other people to get there. So people began to fight."

"Did your father fight too?" I asked, even though I knew that Jonathan would not fight.

"How can Jonathan fight?" Bola asked.

"Papa Paul will never fight anybody," Raliatu said in proud defence of her husband.

"No, sir. Daddy never fought with them," Paul confirmed.

"But why did the police officers on duty and the driver not stop them from fighting?" Bola asked.

"But the two policemen don't stay at the back of the Black Maria. Only we stay at the back. The police stay with the driver in front."

"And when people began to fight and the place was too hot, we shouted and beat the sides of the lorry. We beat the partition between us and the driver that the policemen should come to stop the fight, and also to let air come through. But they ignored us."

"But that's wicked," Bola commented.

"The policemen are very wicked, ma. Very wicked," Paul confirmed. "They treat us like prisoners, whereas we are only suspects."

"How did your father get injured so badly, Paul?" Bola asked.

"It was that mad boy Godwin that started beating him and kicking him. Daddy said Godwin should come away from the window that other people might get air. So he started to abuse Daddy. And I told him not to abuse my Daddy. And he started to fight."

"Did other people not stop him?"

"Everybody was fighting to get to the windows to get air. Some people fell down. That mad Godwin takes Indian hemp. That's why he behaves like that every time."

Paul kept quiet when the Chief Warder came in.

"It is a very bad thing that has happened, sir," he told me, sinking into his chair. He put his cap on the table. "Oga, I have been in prison work for twenty-nine years. I never see a thing like this before."

"It is terrible," I said.

"They say now twenty-seven people have died. I myself counted fifteen with my own eyes. The thing is terrible."

"Paul said there was too much heat and no air in the Black Maria. He said that the people were fighting to get to the windows where they could get air," I told him.

"The Black Maria was too hot. And too many people," the Chief Warder confirmed. "We told government to buy more Black Marias for the prison department. But government said that there was no money."

"But why do the police officers not stay with the suspects at the back of the vehicle, to stop them from fighting?"

"Oga, no policeman will agree to stay at the back of the Black Maria. It is too hot. And the suspects will kill him. I will not deceive you, I cannot stay there myself."

"If the policemen don't stay with the men, how can they hear when the men want assistance?" Bola asked.

"Madam, there's a small window in the partition between the drivers' cabin and the back of the Black Maria. But the suspects trouble the driver too much, so he always shuts the window. The people really give trouble to the driver and the policemen. And the trouble yesterday was due to the big traffic congestion because of the accident on the Mainland Bridge."

"I heard that was quite a bad accident," I said.

"Oga, I hear it was very bad. Seven people killed and thirteen taken to hospital."

"God have mercy," Raliatu cried, in apparent concern for people whose tragedy clearly exceeded hers.

"The Black Maria was trapped in the traffic jam for a long time," the Chief Warder said.

"I see," I said. "Presumably, when the vehicle is in motion there will be some air circulation, however little."

"Oga, you get it. You get it properly. But yesterday the Black Maria stayed in one spot in the traffic jam for a very long time. There was no air in the vehicle. That was the trouble, Oga."

"And no water, no food for the men. That was terrible," Bola commented.

"No water, no food, madam. And no air. That was the trouble, madam. Big trouble. In twenty-nine years I've never seen a thing like this. I pray I never see a tragedy like it again until I retire from government service."

"It is obviously a terrible experience for you and others working here," I observed.

"Oga, it is terrible. Terrible. Terrible. But Oga," the Chief Warder said as if he suddenly remembered something.

"Yes?"

"I want to beg you for something."

"Yes?"

"All the things we've been discussing today, I want you to keep confidential. I beg you not to put any of it in the newspapers."

"What, me? Why d'you think I'd do a thing like that?" I asked.

"Oga, I've always known you are a gentleman. But those newspaper people are bad. You say one thing and they put ten others in their

343

paper. As a civil servant, I must not criticize government in newspaper. I am sure, Oga, you know what I mean," the fat man said, obviously anxious not to be caught doing anything against General Orders, the bible of the public service. "I have now done twenty-nine years in government service. I don't want trouble in the little time that remains before I retire."

TWENTY-FIVE

My friend Police Superintendent Dada expressed the view that the Black Maria tragedy would probably turn out to be a blessing in disguise because it had jolted government into action in response to public outcry. Government had set up a tribunal of inquiry to investigate the disaster.

"I think we need a few more of these disasters to make the public know the terrible things that are happening in certain areas of our public life," the police officer declared. We were both sipping beer after a game of lawn tennis at the Mainland Club three days after the tragedy.

I told him some of the things that Paul had told me when Bola, Raliatu and I visited him at the prison two days before. "I well believe the things Paul said," Dada said. "There are five Black Maria vehicles in the Lagos Metropolitan Area. At any given time at least two, sometimes three of them are broken down. When they are sent to the mechanical workshops you are told there are no spare parts. And you may not take them to outside mechanics. So how can you avoid overcrowding in the Black Maria if the rising number of suspects being kept in custody are to be transported in only one or two Black Maria vans to the courts and back from the courts?"

I took a good draught of beer. I knew the grumbling, frustrated public servant had got another opportunity to attack government.

"Surely something must be done to have better ventilation in the vehicle. Also, at least one or two policemen should stay with the men in the Black Maria to prevent fighting," I observed.

"You see, when the Black Maria is in motion there is air circulation. Also, there is a hatch in the partition between the driver's compartment and the rest of the vehicle."

"So I hear."

"But the driver keeps the hatch perpetually shut for fear of what the suspects can do. And for the same reason, no policeman can stay with them. A number of those suspects are old customers. They can be rough with both police and warder."

"Paul talked of one of the men being an Indian hemp smoker. He said that he started the trouble that led to the disaster," I said.

"If he knew of only one Indian hemp smoker in a crowd of forty-nine suspects, then put him down for an understatement. At least half of those in that van must be on the weed."

"Really? Where do they get it from?"

"From the warders. And from peddlers who take it to them when they come to court. You see all those people milling round the Black Maria and going in and out of the cell in the court premises. A number of them bring the weeds to sell to the boys."

"But do the police escort not see the Indian hemp sellers?"

"Don't ask me, sir. Steward, steward— another two Stars," he ordered. Continuing the conversation, he said: "And those who do not get their supply from the outside get it more expensively from the warders in the prison."

After we had recharged our glasses, my companion asked about Jonathan's progress.

"He's still bad," I told him. "I saw him in the hospital yesterday. When one talks to him, he just nods his head. When he should say 'yes,' he merely nods his head."

"Obviously he hears what you are saying."

"But when he should say 'no,' he still nods his head."

"Really? That's bad. Do the doctors suspect head injury?"

"Maxillino does not think there's head injury."

"He will be alright then."

"I think so too. I only hope he will be well enough to make the 22 October judgment possible. Obviously, the Judge won't deliver the judgment that day if Jonathan, the chief character, is not in court. And he won't be in court if he's not well enough to be discharged from the hospital."

My uncle Papa Ota gave me a small packet to smuggle to Jonathan in the hospital. He told me it was a special preparation from an Imam friend of his. That was three days before the day fixed for the judgment. I took it and lied to my uncle the following day that I had passed it on to Jonathan. I concluded that it was no use arguing with my uncle Papa Ota.

Friday, 22 October 1976: Judgment day in the case of Lagos State versus Jonathan Egbor and Paul Egbor came at last. Jonathan had really not recovered properly, but the doctor discharged him to enable him to go to court to prevent an adjournment. That would have meant more days of suffering for Paul in custody in the prison. The doctor had told me that Jonathan was well enough to go to court and that the knowledge that he was likely to be set free that day would most likely have a salutary effect on his mind.

When I arrived in the court at about ten minutes to nine, I found that all our crowd were already there: Raliatu and the oldest three of her five children; the president and the members of the Esala Progressive Union. They were all there, together with a number of people from the Housing Authority. Our lawyer was already there, together with his junior. Dapo Oladapo Davies was at all times neatly dressed. He was particularly well dressed that day, with his shirt and wing collar looking very white and very well laundered. The State Counsel, Stephen Longson Macaulay, was in his seat, with a young youth corps lawyer at his side. I instinctively hated him for his having been the agent of the suffering that Jonathan and Paul had been subjected to these twenty-one months. But may God forgive me for hating another man whose offence was no more than doing the unpleasant duty for which he was being paid from the taxpayer's money.

The Judge was already in his chambers. I had seen his car parked in the VIP reservation downstairs. The Black Maria had not arrived. Actually, that was nothing serious as the court usually would not start sitting until 9:30 or 10:00.

And my friend Belo was already there too, God bless him. Alex Belo was the man to whom I and all of us supporters of Jonathan Egbor and his son Paul must forever remain grateful for the successful outcome of the case which we expected in a couple of hours. We were now optimistic that we would win. We just had to win.

He and I went downstairs to chat under one of the mango trees while the court awaited the arrival of the Black Maria.

"You think he's going to discharge them?" I asked him.

"Not the slightest doubt in my mind," he said without hesitation. "But, of course, one must make allowance for the human element—what the Judge believes and what he does not believe."

"That human element thing again," I said, visibly annoyed. "But do you think he will believe Jonathan's and Paul's story?"

"I think so. What he really has to determine is whether or not Jonathan and Paul Egbor, or Jonathan singly, or Paul singly, killed Marian Bassey. It was the duty of the prosecution to prove this. And the prosecution has not proved it at all."

"Pity the man did not accept the tape-recording of Nwanna," I said.

"Completely irrelevant now. Oh, by the way, there's this," he said, rubbing the area of the breast pocket in his tweed jacket.

"What's that?" I asked.

"You listen."

I did. "This thing about your being at the murder scene at Sissy Bintu's," Belo's voice issued from the tape-recorder. "Kola here is upset that you wouldn't come forward."

I looked puzzled. "You haven't got it yet?" Belo asked. I shook my head.

"You wait," he said, adjusting the tape to jump a bit of the conversation. Then it started again: "But is it true? That's the point."

"Your voice again," I said.

"You wait," he cautioned.

"True? Of course it is true. Of course it is true that that hemp-smoking boy..."

"M.A. Natural!" I exclaimed. I was most excited at the whole thing. "That's the voice of M.A. Natural," I cried. "You tape-recorded him!"

"Sh-h," Belo cautioned.

"... And I saw it all from her room. Sitting-room, I mean. The boy wielded the thing backwards above his head..."

"You tape-recorded M.A. Natural!" I said again, quite excited.

"Yes, I did. That day he came canvassing for votes for vice-president or something of the Mainland Club, remember?"

"I remember," I said, nodding my head.

"I wasn't really thinking that it would be necessary to put him in the witness box and do with him what we did with Nwanna," Belo chuckled. "I wasn't going to cause him such serious embarrassment. You see, I believe the star witness that died—what was that one's name?"

"Ojerinde," I said.

"I believe Ojerinde had not died at the time. And the need to go to extremes had not yet arisen at that time. But I confess that if the Judge hadn't adopted the attitude he did about Nwanna, I might have considered with you seriously the possibility of treating M.A. Natural the same way we treated Nwanna. We might have had to put M.A. Natural in the witness box and damn the consequences."

"No, no. We couldn't," I declared. "We just couldn't. It would rock Lagos society to its very foundations."

The Black Maria had arrived and Jonathan, Paul and the other occupants of the vehicle had been offloaded. Both Belo and I went to say words of cheer to both of them. Jonathan, as of late, merely nodded his head. Something in the mechanism of that man's mind had been permanently damaged in the Black Maria tragedy; I was certain.

We then went upstairs to the courtroom. We discovered that the Judge had in fact started sitting. He raced through two other cases in which the counsel on both sides were seeking adjournment for one reason or the other. The Judge, to my dismay, in fact spent some time over a third case. He appeared to be in a bad temper that morning, rebuking the police, the prosecuting counsel, the defence counsel and his clerk. I wondered whether this was a taste of things to come. I looked at Raliatu where she sat. I was frightened.

The third case was eventually adjourned, and the Judge announced a short recess after which he retired to his chambers. The recess was very short indeed, as we soon heard the usual three big knocks on the door connecting the court to the judge's chambers. We all stopped the chattering that had been going on and hurried to our places.

The Judge entered, in dignified steps towards his chair, holding a document in his left hand. He had changed to his red robe. He looked full of awe in it. We all knew the awful fact that the wearer of that red robe was vested with the awful responsibility for pronouncing, within an hour from then, that Jonathan Egbor and Paul Egbor should be restored to full liberty, or be hanged by the neck until they be dead, with the cold comfort formula that the Lord should have mercy on their souls.

When he reached his chair, he stopped for a moment and stood still. Then he turned round to face the court. He bowed gravely to all of us standing. He took his seat with dignity. We all sat down.

The clerk called the case number and the title: "Lagos State versus Jonathan Egbor and Paul Egbor. Jonathan Egbor."

Jonathan rose from where he sat with Paul on a bench on which accused persons usually sat. He walked in faltering steps to the dock. He stared at the Judge.

"Paul Egbor," the clerk called.

Paul rose and joined his father in the dock.

There was absolute silence in the court, except for the droning of the air-conditioner in the side wall. We watched the Judge check, sheet by sheet, the document we saw him holding when he came in. He took one dignified look at the two men in the dock. From the dock he looked at the people in the court. He brought out a white handkerchief from the right pocket of his trousers and sneezed into it. He then cleared his throat and began to read his judgment.

He started with a review of the case. He then went on to a summary of the evidence of each of the witnesses on both sides of the case. He started with the first prosecution witness, Bassey Etim Bassey. After spending some five minutes on reading out details of what this witness had taken a whole court day to say, the Judge concluded that the evidence of the first prosecution witness, Bassey Etim Bassey, did not materially assist the court in determining the crucial point: who killed the deceased woman Marian Bassey, if indeed anyone killed her. This was because the witness was himself not present during the affray that led to the death of Marian Bassey. He said that the evidence of the second witness for the prosecution, Elizabeth Akpan, was contradictory to the statement which she had made to the police. In the statement (Exhibit E) she had said that while she saw the beginning of the fight, she left the fight scene early and did not see the point at which one of the combatants allegedly struck down the deceased Marian Bassey. She denied in the statement that she saw anyone wield a weapon. She denied having exclaimed that Gilbert had killed his own mother, as stated by the first defence witness Alex Belo and the first and second accused persons, Jonathan Egbor and Paul Egbor.

My mind started to wander. First, I watched Jonathan in the dock. He stared at the Judge. I believe that he heard what the Judge was saying, but from the way he stared through rather than at him, and from the way he had been behaving strangely since the Black Maria tragedy, I was convinced that he was not following the things which the Judge was saying.

Then I thought of Raliatu. There she sat in the third bench, surrounded by three of her five children, listening to, but obviously not understanding, what the Judge was saying in the judgment that would either set free or condemn to death her husband and her eldest son. I thought of the primary role of reproduction which she had played in her marriage to Jonathan, bearing five children in fifteen years of marriage—a number which could have risen to six had her husband not been forced to a cruel, sexless life in prison custody. I thought of her helplessness in all the tragedy that had overtaken her family; how very little beside her tears she had been able to contribute to the various activities that were being climaxed by the judgment of that day.

The Judge was talking of the fourth prosecution witness, Gilbert Bassey, when my wandering mind left Jonathan and came back to the Judge. "This witness had said at the beginning of his evidence that he neither spoke nor understood the English language. Yet most of the time the witness was in the box, he spoke English in answer to questions put to him by counsel in that language. This, and the demeanour of the witness in the box, made me form the impression that he was not a witness of truth. It is against this background that I do not believe the story of the witness that it was Paul Egbor, the second accused, that wielded the weapon that felled the late Marian Bassey."

The Judge then went into the technicalities of why he admitted the evidence of the first defence witness even though he was not a witness to the fight that allegedly led to the death of Marian Bassey, nor was he able to say that he actually saw who wielded the weapon that allegedly felled the dead woman. The Judge said that the evidence of the second defence witness, Philip Nwanna, to the effect that he stayed in his room all the time that a commotion of the magnitude in which a co-tenant was killed, did not appear to him to be true. He formed the impression that this witness was witness to the fight and that he saw who hit the dead Marian Bassey with a weapon, but that for fear of molestation by the relatives of the deceased woman as alleged by the first defence witness, the witness was not willing to say the truth about this.

My mind again wandered off the subject. I noted that the Judge had taken exactly nineteen minutes from the time he started reading his judgment to that point. The evidence of the four witnesses that had been summarized in nineteen minutes had taken many, many hours of laborious writing by the Judge during three sittings of the court which were spread over so many weeks. And I again asked myself the question why a judge must be subjected to this ordeal of having to take down the evidence of witnesses in his own writing. Why, oh why, do the judiciary in Nigeria refuse to take advantage of developments in electronics? Why don't they tape-record the evidence of witnesses? And why, oh why, must people with cases in court and people in police custody be made to suffer the harsh adverse effects of the refusal of judges and magistrates to tape-record the evidence of witnesses?

My mind wandered further. I was glad that the Judge said he believed that Philip Nwanna was witness to the fight, even though he refused to admit the tape-recording of the conversation in which Nwanna not only admitted this but actually said that Gilbert Bassey wielded the axe handle that hit his mother. From Nwanna my mind went to Sissy Bintu. I remembered that I briefly toyed with the idea of making an inroad into the preserve of my friend M.A. Natural—a thing that must be concealed from my wife Bola. See how Sissy Bintu first raised our hopes over the question of her giving evidence before she later deserted us in our hour of need. And from Sissy Bintu my mind naturally roamed to M.A. Natural, the Pastor's Warden of St. Nicholas Church, the boyfriend of Sissy Bintu—a man committed to the doctrine of "one man, one wife" but who pays the expenses of an apartment for another woman outside the matrimonial home, all to the knowledge of the Pastor of St. Nicholas. But then, where is the Nigerian male that is without sin? Let him step forward and cast the first stone at Martin Abiola, alias M.A. Natural.

"The defence counsel had alleged during the examination of the second prosecution witness that another man, one Emmanuel Ojerinde, who was to have come to give evidence for the defence, had died in a motorcycle accident and that it was this that had made the second defence witness reluctant to come to court and that he had had to be brought by a subpoena. It is pathetic for the defence that they should have been faced with this intolerable situation in a murder case."

Apparently, the Judge was still talking about the evidence of Philip Nwanna. Off went my roaming mind again. I thought of the large number of witnesses to events who later invariably refuse to come forward to give evidence for fear of the harassment of the police and of relatives of accused persons, as well as the fear of the colossal waste of time. I thought of what must be a large number of cases that are being lost all the time by the prosecution for these causes. Then I combined this with the great shortage of able and experienced lawyers to work as state counsel in the Ministry of Justice. When through a combination of these causes a known criminal gets discharged and acquitted, he and his lawyers are carried shoulder-high by his relatives and supporters out of the courtroom. Another criminal has escaped through the gaping holes in our faulty judicial system.

Then I thought of the irony of the particular case of Jonathan and Paul. In the average run of criminal cases, an inexperienced state counsel is matched against a more experienced and able counsel who is defending a person who, in nine out of ten cases, has truly committed the crime for which he is standing trial. But he invariably gets discharged and acquitted due to technicalities and the inadequacies of the prosecution. For every one criminal convicted in a magistrate's or High Court in Lagos, nine others get discharged and acquitted for this cause. Here was the case of Lagos State versus Jonathan Egbor and Paul Egbor. Here these two accused persons had not committed the crime for which they had stood in jeopardy of their lives for these twenty months!

The Judge then summarized the evidence of the first accused person, Jonathan Egbor, and next, that of Paul Egbor. He said that the evidence of each corroborated the evidence of the other. He was, however, not going to rely on this fact to accept as true the story they each told—that it was Gilbert Bassey who wielded an axe handle which was used to strike Marian Bassey and was most probably the cause of her death. He went on to cite a number of legal authorities to explain why he must not accept the evidence of accused persons uncorroborated by any independent witnesses who were actually present at the fight.

I took advantage of my disinterestedness in the long and tedious technical details and the citing of legal authorities, which I did not understand, to look again at Jonathan as he stood in the dock. He appeared even less interested in the proceedings than I was. Still he stared more through the Judge than at him. He certainly understood little or nothing of what that dignitary was saying.

"I have found obvious defects in the case for the defence," I heard the Judge say. I nearly collapsed in my seat. "I however hold that in our legal system it is not the defence that has to prove beyond doubt the innocence of accused persons, but it is the prosecution that has to prove beyond reasonable doubt the guilt of accused persons. I hold that the prosecution has in this case failed to prove beyond reasonable doubt that the first accused person, Jonathan Egbor, or the second accused person, Paul Egbor, or both of them jointly killed the late Marian Bassey."

There was muffled excitement in our ranks. Jonathan and Paul were going to be discharged and acquitted. I immediately looked at them in the dock. There was absolutely no change in the way Jonathan stared through the judge where he stood in the dock. Paul's countenance radiated excitement and happiness.

"I find both the accused persons, Jonathan Egbor and Paul Egbor, not guilty. They are therefore discharged and acquitted."

There were shouts of joy from all parts of the court as we all rose to our feet and made for the dock, in complete disregard of the shouts for order from the court orderly. Paul jumped over the dock rail shouting "Hallelujah, Hallelujah" and ran to the open arms of Raliatu, his mother.

Jonathan Egbor most probably heard the judgment that pronounced him and his son free, but he showed little reaction to it whatsoever. In all probability, he was no longer capable of showing any reaction or emotion to any situation, favourable or adverse. The judgment handed down by the Judge absolved him from guilt for a crime he never committed. It set him free but could never, ever restore the twenty months and twenty-four days of his life that he had lost— partly in police and partly in prison custody. Twenty months and twenty-four days in which he had been cruelly deprived of liberty and the right to live with his family and to move wherever he chose to move in his society.

What the Judge handed down was judgment without justice. It was unfortunately all that he was competent to give in the circumstances of the cumbersome judicial system which he operated. And that judgment had come twenty months and twenty-four days too late to carry with it any viable seeds of justice. Jonathan Egbor had in fact lost the battle for justice from the very day of the fight when cruel fate had placed responsibility for the determination of the truth in the hands of the national police, and of his neighbours at 22 Fasanya Street who were too frightened to come forward to speak the truth. Real justice was impossible under a truth-inhibiting judicial system which had been imported from a foreign clime and which, in spite of over a century of nursing in the inhospitable soil of an indigenous society, has yet, in that society, to grow roots that will reach down to the ground water of true justice.

GLOSSARY

Aladura	Member of a religious sect
Ara-oke	Man from the hinterland
Ashewo	Prostitute
Babalawo	Yoruba for a diviner or doctor
Buba	Yoruba for blouse
Iro	Yoruba for a piece of cloth wrapped round the lower half of a woman to form a skirt
Oga	Master

ABBREVIATIONS

ASP	Assistant Superintendent of Police
DPP	Director of Public Prosecutions
OC	Officer in Charge
P&T	Posts and Telecommunications
PWD	Public Works Department
SP	Superintendent of Police

www.ingramcontent.com/pod-product-compliance
Lightning Source LLC
Chambersburg PA
CBHW071704120626
46550CB00001B/98